Planning Your Financial Future

Planning Your Financial Future

H. STANLEY JONES, *CPA*
Financial Consultant
Jones & Associates
Los Angeles, California 90045

WILEY
John Wiley & Sons
New York • Chichester • Brisbane • Toronto • Singapore

Published by John Wiley & Sons, Inc.

ISBN 0-471-85650-9
ISBN 0-471-63392-5 (pbk.)

Printed in the United States of America

10 9 8 7 6 5 4 3 2 1

To my sons, Hal and Roger, and our grandchildren, to whom the future belongs:

Brian, Elizabeth, Megan, Nicole, Dezary and Philip

Acknowledgments

My thanks to the thousands of individuals in the private, public, academic and nonprofit sectors who have participated in my seminars and classroom activities. They have all helped me to broaden my concepts and approach to render them more personally applicable to an individual's whole life.

I am particularly grateful to Kathryn Reynolds for her dedication and assistance in the preparation of this book.

To my many friends and fellow members of the National Speakers Association who have long encouraged me to put my spoken words in writing to enable more people to learn how they can achieve true personal and financial happiness, I am deeply grateful.

To a mentor whom I did not have the privilege of meeting, that sage soothsayer of the past, that wise, creative inventor, Benjamin Franklin, I am also grateful. I have appreciated his words, wisdom, thoughts and ideas, and have frequently drawn upon his quotations.

Finally, to the many others too numerous to individually name, who, throughout my working and educational years, have contributed to my life's experiences, I express my appreciation and gratitude.

Preface

AN IDEA WHOSE TIME HAS COME

To say that personal financial planning is a totally new concept would not be entirely accurate. In fact, the concept has existed in theory for as long as wealth has been a dream to be pursued and financial independence a goal to be achieved. In practice, however, it wasn't until the early 1980s that this financial strategy finally achieved widespread recognition.

By tracing the origins of what is probably the newest member of the $5-billion-a-year financial consulting industry, we find two primary factors at play: first, an American population caught in the midst of what has appropriately been termed "The Information Age"; and second, an American economy undermined by a staggering national debt as well as frightening inflationary trends and unemployment statistics.

THE INFORMATION AGE

Never before in the history of mankind has so much information been available to so many. With the flick of a switch we can immediately access the latest news on global conflicts, investment trends, medical breakthroughs or even local weather forecasts. Indeed, we are bombarded on a daily basis with more information than we can possibly use in any one lifetime. And to make matters worse, we are often exposed to so many differing viewpoints on the same issue that it is becoming increasingly difficult to determine which elements of the information explosion to use and which to discard.

Consequently, the information age has also become the "advisory" age, ushering in thousands of experts in various fields whose sole task it is to assimilate the unending barrage of information and ultimately disseminate a singular, professional opinion to the oft-confused public. Rather than going through the tedious process of sorting through the available information to hazard educated guesses of our own, we are learning to rely on this growing network of consultants to provide us with advice on everything from sexual proclivities to stock market activities.

ECONOMIC UNCERTAINTY

Since the 1970s, the American public has been presented with a rather strange picture of economic and financial developments. Interest rates have swung from double-digit figures to below 9 percent. Oil supply has run the gamut from feast to famine. The stock market has surged to dizzying new heights and fallen to record lows. In 1987, the stock market broke through the 2000 mark for the first time in history, then crashed over 500 points several months later on October 19, a day now referred to as "Black Monday." Real estate prices have created millions for some and found others selling at a substantial personal loss. Inflation rates have risen and fallen with the economic tides, leaving most Americans constantly perplexed as to whether or not their next salary increase is going to put them ahead or behind in the purchasing game. Unemployment figures have been frighteningly reminiscent of the era of the Great Depression. Economists are predicting that the Social Security system inevitably will go bankrupt. And Congress, after many months of heated debate, has just concluded a sweeping revision of the tax codes.

In addition to all of these confusing trends, we have been faced with a proliferation of investment alternatives ranging from new forms of insurance policies to innovative retirement plans. With even the experts arguing among themselves about bull and bear markets, buy and sell orders, safe bets and sure-fire investments, is it any wonder that the average American feels inadequate when faced with the awesome task of dealing with his or her own financial affairs?

A GENERATION RIPE FOR PERSONAL FINANCIAL PLANNING

Considering the current economic framework in which most Americans are living out their lives, and considering our national tendency to rely on the advice of experts and consultants to sift through the never-ending glut of information now available to us, it is not at all surprising that the personal financial planner has become an important figurehead to the average American family. By providing a step-by-step plan to lead us out of the financial maze in which we now find ourselves, these experts offer to restore our sense of financial balance, and ultimately our peace of mind.

Unfortunately, many of these self-proclaimed experts who have hung our their shingles in recent years have neither the requisite education nor the necessary experience to achieve this end. At present, virtually anyone is entitled to call himself or herself a financial planner. The fact that even the *number* of financial planners currently practicing in this country cannot be pinpointed with any degree of accuracy (estimates vary from 50,000 to over 200,000), is in itself a good indicator of an industry running out of control. To date, millions of dollars have fallen into the hands of con artists masquerading as financial planners. Millions more have been lost due to malpractice by the well intentioned but misinformed.

And even when Congress, in conjunction with state legislators, finally passes more stringent laws governing the conduct and practices of this new body of financial consultants, what guarantees do consumers have that they will be led toward the achievement of lifelong dreams rather than the realization of their worst nightmares?

HOW TO USE THIS BOOK: ADVICE FOR THE CONSUMER OF PERSONAL FINANCIAL PLANNING SERVICES

As potential consumers of personal financial planning, we might all be well advised to consider the wisdom provided by the old tale about the blind men and the elephant. According to the story, depending upon which section of the elephant they touched, each of the blind men drew erroneous conclusions about the size and nature of the beast they were confronting. For example, the one who touched the elephant's trunk incorrectly deduced that the elephant was similar to a large snake while the blind man who touched the elephant's tail falsely assumed that the elephant was more like a small stick. As the moral of this story so aptly suggests, it is impossible to draw accurate conclusions about anything we encounter in life unless we have a complete picture of the whole beast.

The primary reason why people are either dissatisfied with or victimized by personal financial planning is, quite simply, a lack of knowledge about both the process and its practitioners. The bits of information consumers glean from newspapers and magazines are hardly the stuff with which sound financial decisions are made. Like the blind men in the old tale, they have been exposed to only the "trunks" and the "tails" of this financial industry, and have formed rather hasty and often disastrous conclusions about its real nature.

The objectives of this book are to provide you with all of the information you will require to select a competent financial planner and to make better personal financial decisions by taking you through the entire planning process from beginning to end. By knowing exactly what to expect, when to expect it and what to look out for, you will be able to proceed with full confidence in developing a sound plan for your current and future financial resources.

Throughout the book you will also be presented with various exercises designed to increase your awareness of your current and future financial needs. In addition, you will be asked to answer a number of questions regarding your personal objectives and your attitude toward various financial alternatives. Knowing *how* the process works is important; knowing what you *want* from the process is more important still. Far too often a plan which looks good on paper has no value in practice for the simple reason that its emphasis is on the *financial* rather than the *personal* aspects of your life. A good financial plan must lead to the achievement of your life goals, and often these goals are in sharp contrast to more prudent financial decisions. For example, on paper it might be profitable for you to invest your surplus funds in real estate; in practice, however, property management may be an unwelcome hindrance to your current lifestyle. A financial plan should not only make dollars for you; it should also make *sense*.

CONCLUSION

There is no question that personal financial planning is an idea whose time has come. The only question is whether the consumer of this financial product is sufficiently versed in the process to use it wisely and advantageously.

Because each reader's financial circumstances will be unique, we have made no attempt to recommend any specific course of action to be taken. There are hundreds of excellent books that provide detailed descriptions of every conceivable financial product and discussions of which are most suitable for what purpose. Instead, our intention is to provide you with a framework for making sound decisions before, during, and after the financial planning process. Armed with the knowledge in this book, you will be able to select a competent financial planner and work with him or her step by step in mapping out a lifelong program of financial security for you and your family.

Contents

Part 1
Understanding the Process

1
The Objectives of Personal Financial Planning

THE IMPORTANCE OF UNDERSTANDING OBJECTIVES

If you were to poll a thousand people and ask them to define the term "personal financial planning," you would probably hear a thousand different responses. To some, personal financial planning is simply a more comprehensive system of cash management. To others, it is a process centering around some form of tax, estate, or retirement planning. Others still might reply that it has something to do with budgeting or life insurance. And to some degree, they are all correct. Unfortunately, being somewhat correct is what causes consumers of this financial service to be either disappointed or, worse still, devastated by the end results.

Fortunately, we do not have to become experts in this complex financial field in order to become prudent consumers of its products and services. For example, when we hire an electrician to repair a faulty circuit or a plumber to free a stopped drain pipe, we do not need to know exactly how they will go about solving these problems. What we *do* need to know is the specific results we expect to see from their labors. If a light turns on when we touch the switch or if the water drains freely when we turn on the tap, then we can safely assume that the job we have hired these experts to do has been accomplished satisfactorily.

Hiring the expertise of a personal financial planner is basically no different from contracting for the services of an electrician or a plumber. You do not need to have a thorough understanding of the mechanics involved, but you do need to have a clear picture of the results you expect to see. For this reason, it is important to begin our study of personal financial planning with a thorough understanding of what it is *and* what it is not. Only by defining the specific objectives of the process are we able to judge whether or not they have been achieved.

PERSONAL FINANCIAL PLANNING DEFINED

Personal financial planning is a process by which a comprehensive, integrated financial plan is designed to meet the personal objectives of the client through the maximum utilization of all available resources.

While this definition might seem to raise more questions than it answers, by breaking down each of the key words in the phrase we will begin to develop a much clearer sense of the objectives of personal financial planning.

A PROCESS

A personal financial plan addresses your current and future financial condition. In a sense, it is a projection of possibilities or "what ifs" based on potential earnings, investment returns, accumulated assets, predictable expenditures, and personal goals.

Since life is in a constant state of flux and change, a financial plan should never be regarded as being set in concrete. Rather, it must be seen as an ongoing process, a process that must be constantly reviewed, revised, and updated if it is to have any real value in the long-term scheme of things.

COMPREHENSIVE

A meteorologist would never attempt to make a forecast merely by looking out the window to study the cloud formations overhead. He or she would also consult barometric readings, wind patterns, satellite pictures, and all of the other components that ultimately affect weather conditions.

The development of an accurate financial forecast also requires examining data from a variety of sources, including current statements of net worth, insurance policies, existing wills and estate plans, investment portfolios, current income and expenditures, projected income and expenditures, previous years' tax returns, retirement plans, personal goals, attitudes toward risk, and so forth. As with a weather forecast, the more comprehensive and thorough the financial research, the more accurate the predictions will be.

INTEGRATED

To say that the heart is more important to the human body than the kidneys or the lungs more important than the liver could easily be disproved. Remove any one of these vital organs and death would soon ensue. Although the heart, kidneys, lungs, and liver each has an important function to fulfill, none can survive without the efforts of the others.

Just as there are numerous organs required to maintain the health and well-being of your body, so too are there many financial "organs" which must function as a cohesive unit to ensure the health and well-being of your financial condition. The acquisition of certain assets often requires increasing insurance coverages; the buying and selling of investments must be weighed against potential tax consequences; retirement savings plans must be compatible with current lifestyle expenditures. Every element of your financial world must be working in complete harmony if positive results are to be achieved and disastrous outcomes avoided.

MEET THE PERSONAL OBJECTIVES OF THE CLIENT

Money, or the accumulation of wealth, is a means, not an end in itself. In the final analysis, the only true value of money is the extent to which it helps you to achieve your personal goals. For this reason, the critical first step of the financial planning process must be the identification of your current and future objectives. Once these objectives have been identified, each must be assigned its own priority, and a specific plan developed whereby its achievement can be made possible.

Obviously, there will have to be numerous trade-offs and compromises made. It may not be possible to live your current lifestyle *and* achieve your goal of retirement at age 55. However, a personal financial plan will enable you to examine all of the options and possibilities so that priorities can be established and specific steps taken.

MAXIMUM UTILIZATION OF ALL AVAILABLE RESOURCES

By the term "resources" we are actually referring to two different things. First, of course, are your financial resources. Making your money work as hard for *you* as you work for *it* is one of the primary objectives of the financial plan.

The second meaning of the word resources is the expertise

available to you through financial planning. By consulting with experts in the field of risk management, investments, tax laws, estate and retirement planning, your financial planner brings a wealth of knowledge to the effective management of your financial affairs.

CONCLUSION

In summary, following are the primary objectives which can and should be met through personal financial planning:

1. Thorough review of current financial situation
2. Projections of future financial condition
3. Continual revisions and update to the financial plan based on changes in market conditions, tax laws, personal circumstances, and so on
4. Thorough review of all factors affecting your financial condition including:
   a. Insurance policies and medical plans
   b. Retirement plans/pension funds
   c. Investment portfolio
   d. Current assets and liabilities
   e. Previous years' tax returns
   f. Current will/trusts/estate plans
   g. Current income and expenditures
   h. Projected income and expenditures
5. The identification of specific attitudes toward risk and various investment alternatives
6. The identification and prioritization of your personal goals
7. The outlining of specific steps to be taken for the achievement of your personal goals

8. The careful coordination of all factors affecting your personal financial condition
9. The maximum utilization of all available financial resources including cash, assets, and leverage
10. The maximum utilization of expertise from a variety of financial fields

IS PERSONAL FINANCIAL PLANNING FOR YOU?

Now that you have a thorough understanding of the objectives of personal financial planning, the only question that remains is whether you would benefit from this unique service.

The following questionnaire was designed to help you to make this important decision. Hopefully, by taking an objective look at both the dollars and the sense of personal financial planning in terms of your current and future financial needs, you will be able to reach the appropriate conclusion.

The Dollars

Scoring Key

In the space provided, write the point value of your answer to each of the questions as indicated by the following chart.

Answer	Point Value
Yes	0
No	1
Don't Know	2

_____ 1. Did less than 20 percent of your gross income go toward the payment of income tax last year?

_____ 2. Do you plan your taxes all year round?

_____ 3. Do you have a method of sheltering current income to minimize your tax burden other than your home mortgage or IRA?

_____ 4. Do you make maximum deposits to your IRA or Keogh plan every year?

_____ 5. Do you and your spouse earn a combined income of less than $50,000?

_____ 6. Is your investment portfolio sufficiently diversified?

_____ 7. Do you make maximum use of leverage to fund investments?

_____ 8. Do you have a specific investment plan or strategy to follow?

_____ 9. Is your investment strategy consistent with your current and long-range financial goals?

_____ 10. When selecting your investments, are you fully aware of all potential risks and tax consequences?

_____ 11. Based on your tax bracket for last year's income tax returns, did the effective rate of return on all of your investments equal or exceed the inflation rate?

_____ 12. Will you have sufficient funds to send your children to the college of their choice?

_____ 13. Have you reviewed the insurance coverage on your personal property within the last 24 months?

14. Could your family financially survive the following situations without having to drastically alter your current standard of living or future goals?

_____ a. Premature death of principal wage earner

_____ b. Family member required to undergo surgery and treatment for cancer

_____ c. Total disability of principal wage earner

_____ d. Total loss of family residence and personal possessions due to electrical fire

_____ e. Being sued for $1 million by a couple whose eldest son was killed when you ran a red light in your car

_____ 15. Do you have a contingency fund equivalent to six months' wages in cash or liquid assets?

_____ 16. Do you have a current will?

_____ 17. Will your entire estate pass tax-free to your heirs?

_____ 18. Do you understand the estate tax consequences of the ownership of life insurance policies?

_____ 19. Do you understand the benefits and disadvantages of both living and testamentary trusts?

_____ 20. Have you appointed legal guardians for children who have not yet reached the age of majority?

_____ 21. Have you made provisions for the management of your affairs in the event that you should become mentally incompetent either through accident or illness?

_____ 22. Have you named contingent beneficiaries on all of your insurance policies?

_____ 23. Would your family know where to find all important personal and financial documents in the event of sudden death or incapacitation?

_____ 24. Are you setting aside a sufficient percentage (5–10 percent) of your income each year to fund a comfortable retirement?

_____ 25. Do you have a current statement of net worth?

_____ 26. Are your total current fixed and variable monthly expenses (not including mortgage payments on your family residence) less than 30 percent of your take-home pay?

_____ 27. Are you saving at least 10 percent of your gross (pretax) income every year?

_____ 28. Are your payments on credit cards and other forms of installment debt (not including mortgage payments on your family residence) less than 20 percent of your take-home pay?

_____ 29. Do you have a *written* personal budget or gameplan for your monthly income?

_____ 30. Do you know the approximate amount of discretionary income you will have to work with in the next five years?

_____ **Subtotal**

The Sense

Scoring Key

In the space provided, write the point value of your answer to each of the questions as indicated by the chart below.

Answer	Point Value
Yes	0
No	2

_____ 1. Are you willing to invest approximately 5 percent of your current income for the development of a personal financial plan and at least 1 percent of your future annual income for the continued maintenance of the plan?

_____ 2. Does your current financial situation allow you to lead the kind of lifestyle you would want for yourself and your family?

_____ 3. Do you understand all of the fine print in your insurance policies?

_____ 4. Do you have a thorough understanding of all of the various forms of investments currently available to you? (Stocks, bonds, mutual funds, limited partnerships, futures contracts and options, etc.)

_____ 5. Do you have a written list of personal and financial goals?

_____ 6. Do you have a written plan for achieving those goals?

_____ 7. Do you feel that you are firmly in control of your current financial situation?

_____ 8. Are you and your spouse always in total agreement about the management of your finances?

_____ 9. Are you confident about your financial future?

_____ 10. Are you able to sleep at night without worrying about the soundness of your financial decisions?

_____ 11. Are you able to fill out loan documents and credit applications without having to stretch the truth a little?

_____ 12. Are you able to save as much money as you would like?

_____ 13. Do you have complete confidence in all of your current financial advisors? (Accountant, stockbroker, banker, insurance agent, estate attorney, trustee, etc.)

_____ 14. Do you feel that you are currently paying the minimal amount of tax possible on your personal income?

_____ 15. Do you feel confident that you will be able to enjoy a comfortable retirement without having to budget or restrain your expenditures severely?

_____ 16. Do you have total peace of mind regarding all of your current and future financial matters?

_____ **Subtotal**

_____ **Subtotal from "Dollars" questionnaire**

_____ **TOTAL SCORE**

INTERPRETING THE RESULTS OF THE QUESTIONNAIRE

40 or more — Personal financial planning is a must! Your answers indicate an uncertainty about your financial affairs which can only lead to highly unsatisfactory consequences.

29 to 39 — A thorough review of your personal finances is definitely in order. You should consider personal financial planning as a means of getting your financial affairs firmly on the right track within the next 12 to 24 months.

10 to 24 — Although many aspects of your personal finances are well under control, there are some very obvious gaps which need to be examined closely. Whether or not personal financial planning is required depends on your ability to find competent financial advisors and your willingness to spend the necessary time to coordinate their activities.

0 to 9 — Congratulations! On the whole, you seem to have a very good handle on your financial affairs. Personal financial planning probably would be an

unnecessary expense at this time. However, you should pay close attention to the questions that revealed a bit of uncertainty or lack of vigilance in your current plan. Left unattended, these matters could create future problems.

Now that we have determined the specific objectives of personal financial planning and the extent to which it might be of value to you, let's turn our attention to the people behind the process.

2
Selecting Your Personal Financial Planner

THE ROLE OF THE PERSONAL FINANCIAL PLANNER

If there is one factor more than any other that ultimately will affect the results you obtain through personal financial planning, it is the selection of your financial planner. Since the process is only as effective as its practitioners, great care must be taken to find a planner who is competent, thorough, professional, and above all else, sincerely interested in your financial well-being.

In a sense, the financial planning process is very similar to a football game. It takes a combination of financial muscle and clever strategy to score against an opposing team consisting of such determined players as Inflation, Taxation, and Risk. Following through on this analogy, the financial planner is like the quarterback of your team. It is his or her task to devise game-winning strategies by studying the moves of the opposition and using all available financial muscle to full advantage. Whether you win, lose, or draw in this important match will depend to a large degree on the skills of the quarterback you select.

THE SKILLS OF YOUR QUARTERBACK

Virtually every member of the financial industry has jumped on the financial planning bandwagon within the last decade. Bankers, lawyers, insurance agents, accountants, and stockbrokers alike are now proudly waving the personal financial planning banner from their front doorsteps. "Look what we have to offer now!" they clamor in unison. And looking, *carefully* looking, is where your job begins. Like a professional football team that sends out scouts to judge the quality of players at various college campuses, as potential consumers of personal financial planning you must do your own selective scouting to determine the quality of the players in the various financial fields.

Basically, all personal financial planners can be categorized into three distinct groups based on methods of compensation for services rendered. By studying the differences among these three groups and determining which of the three offers the services you need at the price you are prepared to pay, you will be able to narrow your search from the hundreds of possibilities to a handful of probabilities. Most important of all, by knowing the strengths and weaknesses of your quarterback *before* you begin the game, you will be in a much better position to compensate for any perceived weaknesses by adding additional players to the team.

Fee Planners

As the name suggests, fee planners work on a fixed or flat fee basis. The amount charged generally ranges from $500 to $5000 or more, depending on the complexity of your financial affairs. How those fees are determined varies from planner to planner. Some planners bill on an hourly basis ($50–$125 an hour). Still others work on a fixed percentage (.5–2 percent) of either your current income, current net worth, and/or current assets. The reputation, education, and experience of the planner may also affect the price.

The most obvious drawback to engaging the services of a fee planner is that it can be a very expensive process. In fact, to many families such services are, quite simply, cost prohibitive. However, these financial planners justify the expense by pointing out three factors. First, their fees are not out of line with the hourly rates charged by other professionals such as psychologists, doctors, marriage counselors, or even interior designers. Second, because they are members of a highly regarded group of professionals, these planners may bring more experience and education to the process, as well as the stringent rules and regulations that govern the practices and ethical conduct of their profession, than the others do. Third, considering all of the financial services the client receives from the process (a current will, the establishment of trust funds, the preparation of cash-flow and personal financial statements, and insurance counseling) the *one* bill from the financial planner is certainly far less than the total of *all* of the bills a client would receive if he or she were to consult an accountant, attorney, trustee, and investment advisor on an individual basis to provide the same services.

Another charge that is often leveled at fee planners is that they tend to let the ball drop at the 10-yard line. Since they are guaranteed financial compensation regardless of the outcome of the process, fee planners may be less aggressive when it comes to making sure that clients actually *implement* the recommendations of the plan. Whether you buy the necessary life insurance, establish that trust fund for your children, or invest your surplus funds in the recommended tax shelters has no effect whatsoever on the planner's pocketbook. And where there is no obvious financial gain, there often can be professional neglect. Because of the natural human tendency to procrastinate, this *can* make for a very disastrous combination.

By the same token, the fact that fee planners do *not* receive a commission when financial products are purchased is a very strong plus. Many claim this makes these planners less biased in the advice they give and more objective in the recommendations they make. It should be remembered, however, that while the planner may not be receiving *direct* compensation for the insurance you are advised to purchase or the trustee you are advised to deal with, there may be some measure of *indirect* compensation taking place. The financial industry has a very active underground network. It is quite possible that *somebody's* brother-in-law will benefit from your purchases or that *somebody's* client list will grow because of a gentlemen's agreement regarding client referrals.

This is not to say that you must be constantly second-guessing the motives of the fee planner; it is merely to suggest that you should never be lulled into a false sense of security when decision time rolls around. It is your plan, your money, and your future; and ultimately which products you buy and whose services you employ will be entirely your choice.

Commission Planners

If you are looking for a low-cost alternative to personal financial planning, then you definitely will want to investigate the services of planners who function in this category. Unlike their fee-charging associates, commission planners often do the job for free. Rather than paying these planners directly, you compensate them for their services *indirectly* when you purchase the various financial products they recommend.

Many would argue that although the commission planner seems to offer cost-free services in the short term, the ensuing years will find clients paying far more than they bargained for. Since this planner benefits directly when specific stocks and insurance policies are purchased or when monies are invested in recommended tax shelters, limited partnerships, mutual funds, and pension plans, some degree of bias is ever present. For this reason, clients may find themselves purchasing far more insurance than they actually require or investing hard-earned dollars in funds that produce only minimal results.

Unlike the fee planners who sometimes fail in the implementation department, commission planners are very thorough in this area—for obvious reasons. If the client doesn't follow through, the planner doesn't get paid. By the same token, there is a tendency for some commission planners to leave the game after the first touchdown. It should be remembered that financial planning is a process, not a one-time purchase of products and services. When circumstances change, your planner should be on hand to revise and modify your plan to reflect those changes.

It also has been suggested that many commission planners lack the necessary education and experience that the personal financial planning process requires. Certainly a large number of these so-called planners are little more than insurance salespeople and stockbrokers with a new title on their business cards. However, it should also be recognized that many commission planners have undergone intensive training to upgrade their professional skills and knowledge.

Fee-Plus-Commission Planners

Fee-plus-commission planners can offer you the best or worst of both worlds. Ideally, they provide the expertise of the fee planner at a considerably lower cost, while at the same time maintaining the commission planner's emphasis on follow-through and implementation.

Since part of their compensation comes in the form of commission sales, they also bring with them the same potential for bias, oversell, and neglect of the necessary long-term maintenance of the plan.

In summary, Table 2–1 offers another look at the strengths and weaknesses of each of these three categories of financial planners:

Table 2–1
Comparison of Financial Planners

Category	Strengths	Weaknesses
Fee	Expertise/education Professionalism Emphasis on continual maintenance of plan	Offer little or no emphasis on implementing plan Biases may be more subtle More expensive
Commission	Free services Usually highly knowledgeable in one or more aspects of financial planning Emphasis on implementing plan	Obvious biases Tend to oversell Offer little or no emphasis on plan maintenance
Fee + Commission	Low-cost expertise Emphasis on implementing plan Some degree of ongoing maintenance of plan	Product biases Potential for oversell May lack specific expertise

As Table 2–1 indicates, regardless of the method of compensation used, all planners have distinct advantages and obvious limitations to offer to their clients. Our purpose here is not to state that one is better than another; indeed, it would be foolhardy to make such sweeping conclusions about *any* group of professionals. There are good and bad doctors, dentists, teachers, and social workers just as there are competent and incompetent personal financial planners. In the final analysis, the type of planner you use must be based on the following factors:

1. The money you are prepared to invest in the process, and;
2. Your personal assessment of the planner.

THE MONEY YOU ARE PREPARED TO INVEST IN THE PROCESS

Throughout this book we will constantly refer to personal financial planning as an investment to be made rather than an expense to be paid. The reason for this will become more apparent in subsequent chapters as we begin to explore financial planning in greater detail. Hopefully, however, the overview we have already given of this process is helping you develop a sense of its long-range potential to create wealth as surely as any other form of investment would. Properly conceived, thoroughly implemented, and diligently maintained, a personal financial plan will grow in value over time, producing both intrinsic and extrinsic rewards for many years to come.

Unlike the preparation of a personal will or a federal tax return, a financial plan is neither a moral nor a legal requirement. Nonetheless, it is rapidly becoming a twentieth century necessity for long-term financial security and peace of mind. With so many investment alternatives to choose from, with inflation steadily eroding the future purchasing power of personal income, with frequent revisions to tax codes, and unending interest rate fluctuations, the average American family seems to be trapped some place between the proverbial rock and the hard spot. Our choice is either to try to keep pace with the constant changes by becoming our own self-appointed planners or to invest in the services of competent expertise to lead us safely through this financial maze. Although the investment you will be required to make will vary depending on your financial needs and the type of planner with whom you elect to work, you will probably need to consider making an investment of approximately 5 percent of your current gross income for the initial development and implementation of the plan, and approximately 1 percent a year thereafter to maintain the plan. For example, if you and your spouse together earn $50,000, then your initial investment will be somewhere in the neighborhood of $2500 with an annual maintenance fee of approximately $500.

If this amount seems staggering, take a moment to consider all of the other things on which we spend our money—things that have a limited life span and a limited impact on our financial well-being. Using our example of the couple whose gross income is $50,000, their financial plan would cost only twice as much as a new sofa and less than 20 percent of the total price tag for a second car. In the final analysis, the question that needs to be answered is: How much is financial security and total peace of mind worth to you and your family? Considering all that personal financial planning has to offer, the required investment is minimal by comparison. As someone wisely cautioned, if you think the price for financial planning is expensive, wait until you get the bill for *not* planning.

Even if you are reluctant to invest a considerable amount in financial planning right away, you can always make use of the services of a commission planner. Since you are under no obligation to purchase any of the products he or she recommends, you could conceivably receive a considerable amount of free counsel. However, if you decide to implement the plan, a substantial investment still will be required. There will be insurance policies to purchase, funds to invest, professionals (such as a lawyer to write your will) to hire, and so forth. No matter how you approach it, a considerable investment must be made in your financial future.

Since this is an investment, you can expect some tangible financial results. A good financial plan should provide a quick payback on your investment. A $2000 or $3000 planning fee is often returned to you in the form of tax savings or increased net worth within the ensuing 12 to 24 months. While you may be required to purchase additional insurance, a good planner can often save you money on your existing policies so that additional coverage can be purchased for little or no more than you are currently spending for limited coverage. Most important of all, you will be able to proceed with your life without those doubts and worries about your financial future. It is a small price to pay for a good night's sleep, is it not?

YOUR PERSONAL ASSESSMENT OF THE PLANNER

As we said earlier, the selection of your personal financial planner is probably the most important factor that determines the quality of your financial plan. We have examined the three broad categories of financial planners; now it is time to get down to the specifics within those categories to help narrow the field.

The following questionnaire was designed to enable you to make this final selection with confidence and with ease. As you will see, there are two primary areas for your consideration. The "Dollars" concentrates on the practical aspects of the selection process while the "Sense" focuses on the emotional or subjective issues that come into play. Even though a planner may have all of the professional qualifications you are looking for, he or she may still be an unsuitable candidate because of a personality flaw. You must have confidence in the planner both as a professional *and* as a person for the process to work well.

It is imperative that you get a thorough answer to each of these important questions. You need to be as blunt and direct in your examination of the financial planner as a prosecuting attorney would be of a criminal on the witness stand. The person on trial in your courtroom is someone who has the capacity to lead you to total financial devastation if he or she should prove to be selfishly motivated or unqualified for the task at hand. This is no time for you to feel shy about asking or hesitant about prying. Remember, your financial future may be at stake.

The Dollars: Key Questions to Ask the Planner

1. Is financial planning a full-time occupation or a part-time endeavor for the planner?

   If financial planning is a part-time endeavor for the planner, then you should probably end the interview right here. Personal financial planning is a very complex process. It requires a high level of expertise and an intense dedication on the part of the planner. In our opinion, those who practice this profession on a part-time basis or as a sideline to their principal occupation cannot give the necessary time and attention to your financial affairs.

2. How long has this individual been providing financial planning services?

   Generally, the more experience the planner has the better the results will be. Try to find someone who has at least two years' experience in this field.

3. What previous experience has the planner had with clients in your age/income bracket?

   The quality of the planner's experience is often more important than the quantity. If the planner is used to dealing with clients whose net worth is in the $500,000 to $1 million range and your current net worth is less than $100,000, you may find yourself dealing with someone who is well versed in estate trusts and tax shelters but who doesn't have enough practical experience in matters pertaining to your specific needs.

4. Will the planner be receiving commissions or other forms of compensation if you purchase a specific financial product or agree to use the financial services he or she recommends?

   Again, there is no reason to avoid dealing with a product-oriented planner. Just be aware of the potential for bias and oversell. Planners are required by law to inform clients of any commissions or other forms of compensation they might receive if certain products or services are purchased.

5. What proof will the planner offer that the investments and/or tax shelters being recommended are:
   a. legal?
   b. financially sound?
   c. offer the best rate of return?
   d. offer the best tax advantages?

A good planner will provide this information as part of the service. If you have any doubts about the investments being recommended you should consult the Securities Exchange Commission (SEC), and/or any of the recognized investors' references such as *Barron's, Moody's,* or *Standard & Poor's.*

6. What proof will the planner offer that the insurance being recommended is the most economical or practical?
   The planner should be prepared to discuss the alternatives as well as to document the reasons why the policy being recommended is the most suitable. You may want to consult recent editions of *Best's Life Reports, Best's Insurance Management Reports* or *Who Writes What in Life and Health Insurance.* Each of these references provides up-to-date information on the various types of insurance policies as well as the financial integrity of the insurance companies that underwrite them.

7. Is the financial planner licensed with the SEC?
   Although licensing is not yet a professional requirement, it is a legal requirement for those planners who intend to provide investment advice to their clients as an integral part of their services.

8. How does the firm/planner rate in terms of reputation?
   Ask for at least three references. Then be sure to contact the individuals personally. Find out how long they have known the planner, how they came to use his or her services, their personal observations of the planner (strengths and weaknesses), and why they would recommend him or her to you. You might also ask each of these three people to provide you with one or two names of their own, that is, other people they know who have used the services of this planner/firm. Obviously, the planner is not going to give you the names of dissatisfied custom-

ers. However, if you do a little research on your own, you may come across someone who has had a less than favorable experience.

9. What kind of experience/expertise does the firm/planner have in *all* areas of financial planning?

   Your accountant may be a wizard at tax matters, but may not know the first thing about insurance. Your insurance agent may be tops in the field, but may not have enough practical experience in estate planning. Obviously, every financial planner has his or her area of expertise; however, in order for the plan to be truly effective, you must be certain that you will be receiving expert guidance in *all* financial areas.

10. Does the planner have any special education and/or qualifications for providing personal financial planning services?

    Since personal financial planning is a relatively new field, there are only a handful of institutions currently offering degree programs to potential practitioners. The following designations will help you evaluate the special education and/or qualifications of the planner:

    ChFC Chartered Financial Consultant
    A degree program offered by the American College in Bryn Mawr, Pennsylvania.

    CFP Certified Financial Planner
    A self-study program offered by the College for Financial Planning in Denver, Colorado.

    IAFP International Association of Financial Planners
    This designation indicates a membership, not a college degree.

    Be sure to ask your planner about his or her educational background. Although the majority of colleges are not yet offering full degree programs in the field, many now include personal financial planning as part of the curriculum in other degree programs.

11. Does the firm/planner work with outside consultants in developing the financial plan?

    If so, who are they and what are *their* professional qualifications?

12. Will you have the opportunity to meet with these outside consultants personally?

    If you have a particular question about some aspect of your plan, you will want to be able to talk directly to an expert in the field.

13. Ask to see a copy of a completed financial plan.

    This will be a good indicator of the type of service the planner intends to provide. Most reports are generated by a computer and consist primarily of financial data. However, these facts should be given in response to the client's personal goals and attitudes. Reading through the plan will help you to develop a sense of whether the information it contains is based as much on subjective data as it is on dollars and cents. A good financial plan is one that is developed in response to personal feelings and not just financial facts.

14. Ask for a written agreement that clearly states the fee you will be charged *and* the specific services to be provided.

    Before you sign on the dotted line, be sure you have a written description of the services the planner intends to provide. In this way you will have a clear and measurable set of objectives against which you can weigh the results you actually received. Also be sure the agreement clearly states the terms and conditions regarding payment for services rendered in the event you are dissatisfied with the final product (i.e., the plan itself), or if you become disenchanted with the process or the planner along the way. Verbal promises are quickly given and all too quickly forgotten.

15. Ask for a written agreement that clearly states the fee you will be charged for annual maintenance of your financial plan as well as the specific services that will be provided.

    Will the maintenance fee include the preparation of tax returns? How much free consultation time does the fee include? How often will the plan be reviewed throughout the year? If major changes are required, will the maintenance fee cover these revisions?

16. Ask the planner to describe in detail exactly how the planning process works.

    Better still, ask the planner to commit this description to writing. Having a clear sense of how the planner intends to develop your financial plan will provide you with a good set of checks and balances by which to measure the progress and overall results.

17. How much time will the planner spend with you and your spouse in private consultation?

    As you will see in the following chapter, the planner should be prepared to spend a considerable amount of private time with you and your spouse at various stages throughout the process.

The Sense: Key Questions To Ask Yourself

1. Is the planner interested primarily in providing you with financial services or selling you financial products?
2. Does this planner inspire your confidence?
3. Would you feel comfortable revealing personal financial data to this individual?
4. Would you feel comfortable discussing personal goals, family circumstances, and so forth with this individual?

5. Does the planner appear to have a genuine concern about your financial well-being and your family?
6. Is the planner someone you would be comfortable associating with over an extended period of time?
7. Do you feel as though a high-pressured sales pitch is being directed at you?
8. Does the planner conduct himself or herself in a professional manner?
9. Does the planner spend more time listening *to* you than talking *at* you?
10. Are you ready to take the plunge?

THE EFFECTIVENESS OF YOUR COACHING SKILLS

At the beginning of this chapter we outlined the two important factors that will affect the results you obtain from personal financial planning. The first was the selection of the personal financial planner who will play the all-important position of quarterback, calling the shots and directing the plays.

The other factor we mentioned was the effectiveness of your coaching skills. Even though you will remain on the sidelines throughout most of the process, like any good coach your impact must be felt on the field during play if your team is to emerge victorious. The following chapter will outline how you can have a positive impact on the outcome of your financial plan.

3
The Nine Stages of the Personal Financial Planning Process

COACHING YOUR PERSONAL FINANCIAL PLANNING TEAM

Even though you may not have the requisite knowledge and experience to participate in the game itself, you can still play an active role by monitoring the activities of your financial planning team. Obviously, the more familiar you are with the rules of the game and the way in which it should be played, the more effective you will be at coaching the players. By way of preparation, then, let's begin by examining the nine stages of the personal financial planning process.

The Selling of the Concept

Our first introduction to the concept of personal financial planning is usually some form of subtle sales technique. Free seminars, color brochures, emotionally charged advertisements, personal letters, or telephone appeals are all popular methods for capturing out initial interest and setting the stage for encouraging us to become consumers of financial planning services.

Although we like to think of ourselves as prudent consumers, in truth, most of our buying decisions are the result of emotional rather than logical conclusions. Think for a moment about some of the major purchases you have made in the last few years—your current automobile or home, for example. We can tell ourselves all we like that we bought the car because it has an excellent fuel economy rating or a five-year factory warranty. However, if the same features had been available at half the price for a car that looked like a WWII army tank (right down to the color of the paint) would you have bought it? Probably not.

By the same token, didn't we all justify the purchase of our new home with words like, "It was a good deal . . . it has excellent resale value . . . the wall-to-wall carpeting is in like-new condition." However, if the same house had been available for a fraction of the price in a much less desirable neighborhood, would you have changed your mind and purchased the lower priced house? Not likely.

If we were to be totally honest, the real reason we bought that particular automobile and that particular house was because of the way they made us feel. Something about the car and the home triggered a positive emotional response somewhere deep inside us. All we had to do then was to find enough logical reasons to support the emotional decision we had already made, reasons like "good deal," "fuel economy," or "good resale value."

A good salesperson knows that people buy primarily because of feelings, not facts; and many personal financial planners are good salespeople. Take a closer look at those clever advertisements or those free seminars for personal financial planning and what you will find is a strong underlying theme of emotional appeals. "Do it for your children. Do it for your peace of mind. Do it to become wealthy. Do it for your spouse. Do it so you can enjoy an early retirement." To invest in a financial plan out of a sense of duty to your family or because of current apprehensions or future promises is not necessarily a bad idea. Why do we pursue money if not to satisfy some deep-rooted emotion within us? And why do we "buy" if not in response to an inner emotional urging?

The decision to invest in a personal financial plan is almost always an emotional decision, which is why great caution must be exercised. This is also the reason why the next step in the process is probably one of the most crucial phases. It is here that emotion must be kept at bay in order for logic to have sufficient room to operate.

The Initial Interview

As the title suggests, the purpose of this phase in the process is to give you a chance to interview the financial planner in a private, one-on-one session. This is where the list of questions we provided in Chapter 2 must be asked and answered. You should come away from this session with a clear sense of:

1. The exact nature of the services the planner intends to provide.
2. The fee to be charged for those services.
3. An outline of the product you will be receiving, that is, a sample financial plan.
4. How quickly you can expect to see a return on your investment whether in terms of an increased net worth or a decreased tax burden.
5. The qualifications of the planner.
6. The qualifications of the experts he or she will be consulting in the development stages of your financial plan.
7. Names of other clients who have used the planner's services who can be contacted as references.

8. The focus of the planner (selling products or providing services).
9. How the planner intends to keep your plan up-to-date in the years ahead as well as the fees involved for this maintenance service.
10. The personality of the planner. (Is this someone you can trust? Feel comfortable working with over the years? Is this someone who inspires your confidence?)

Although the planner will probably want to get a firm commitment from you at the end of this session, you should delay that commitment until you have:

1. Had a chance to check out the planner's references thoroughly.
2. Had a chance to weigh the decision carefully.
3. Received a *written* proposal from the planner clearly outlining all of the specific details discussed in this interview.

Gathering the Facts: Empirical Data

Once the decision to engage the services of a personal financial planner has been made, the next step is to assemble all of the facts, figures, and documents that collectively make up your current financial state of affairs. Generally, the financial planner will ask you to complete a questionnaire similar to the one found in Chapter 4. He or she may also ask for copies of insurance policies, your will, bank statements, tax returns, and so forth, to help develop a more comprehensive profile of your financial situation.

Be forewarned that this can be a very time-consuming and tedious process. In fact, you may be tempted to give up halfway through or to skip over some of the questions. However, being thorough and accurate in the completion of the questionnaire is crucial to the success of your plan.

Working through the questionnaire and assembling the necessary documents may not be much fun, but it can certainly be very revealing. Having to hunt through bottom drawers, old shoe boxes, and office filing cabinets to find important pieces of information gives you a good idea of the turmoil your family would experience if you were to die unexpectedly. Although we all agree that it would be a good idea to buy one of those family financial record books which schedules assets and personal property, and lists the location of all important financial documents as well as the names and addresses of financial advisors, how many of us actually buy one, or for that matter, keep it up-to-date?

Another revealing aspect of the process occurs for most people when they actually sit down (many of them, for the first time) to list their fixed and variable expenses. When you discover that you are spending more each month on your country club membership than you are on food for the family table, or that your family's "second" income is actually costing more than it brings in by the time you add up taxes, lunches, babysitters, housekeepers, transportation, and clothing allowances, it may encourage you to take a harder look at how you have been managing (or mismanaging) your personal finances all these years.

Although there is no easy way to get the fact-gathering process done, there are a few things you can do to minimize the hassle. First, a few phone calls to your family lawyer, accountant, banker, stockbroker and insurance agent can save you a lot of unnecessary aggravation. Your current financial advisors have copies of most of the documents you will need (divorce or marital agreements, will, tax returns, stock portfolio, insurance policies, loans, pension plans, etc.) and are usually willing to send you photocopies at no charge.

Second, it may be possible for your financial planner to assemble much of the data by having you sign a simple release letter that will advise your lawyer, banker, and so forth that you wish them to release specific facts or documents to the financial planner on your behalf.

Third, your check register and credit card statements will make determining your monthly expenditures fairly easy and relatively accurate. Simply take the total payments you have made for various items over the last three months and divide that total by three to get a monthly average.

Fourth, if you are employed by a company, find out who is in charge of the various benefits plans. In a large firm it will be someone in the personnel department; in a smaller firm it is often the office manager. Ask this individual to provide you with copies of all company-sponsored medical, dental, retirement, and/or profit-sharing plans in which you are participating.

Finally, don't try to do it all in one night or in an all-weekend blitz. Set aside a little time each day over a two-week period to get the facts down on paper. Working on this project for 20 or 30 minutes daily will make it seem less burdensome than trying to do it all at once. Also, you will be far more likely to do a thorough job when you give yourself adequate time and breathing space than if you tried to labor through it in a single session.

Gathering the Facts: Subjective Information

After reviewing your completed questionnaire, the planner should schedule a private session with you (and your spouse, whenever possible) to assemble additional data. Unlike the facts gathered by the questionnaire, the purpose of this meeting is to develop a clear list of the personal goals you wish to achieve through financial planning as well as to define your attitude toward various forms of investments, trusts, and other financial media.

In preparation for this session, you and your spouse should take the time to actually write down your personal goals in each of six important areas: family, current lifestyle, current financial condition, retirement, estate disposition and other areas of concern. (In Chapter 7 you will find a more thorough description of each of these categories, as well as specific guidelines for developing your goal lists.)

One of the things we strongly recommend is that both spouses prepare the lists individually. In this way, neither will be swayed by the opinions or the objectives of the other. Then, when your individual lists are complete, sit down together and develop a final list that will be the one you will actually take into the planning session. This list will, of course, reflect a combination of individual goals and collective compromises.

Remember, it may not always be possible to achieve *all* of your goals. In fact, many of your goals may prove to be obstacles to the achievement of other objectives on your list. You may not, for example, be able to fund your children's education *and* purchase a new home within the next 10 years. For this reason, we also recommend that you establish priorities for each goal on your list. If something has to give way, what would it be? Which of the goals are most important to you? And which of the goals are least important to you?

The financial planner should also spend part of this session determining your attitudes toward various financial media, and whenever possible, helping you to understand the differences, the advantages, the drawbacks, and the soundness of each of these forms of investment. More often than not, our attitudes toward various investments are colored by either past experiences (personal or second-hand) or lack of information. To some, the term "tax shelter" implies something that is risky and illegal. Others have been conditioned to believe that government bonds are the best and safest forms of investment. To some a house is where you raise your family; to others, it is nothing more than a short-term tax shelter with long-term profit potential. The planner's task in determining your attitude toward various forms of investments is to understand and educate as well as to appreciate and inform.

One of the most important areas for discussion with your

planner will be your attitude toward risk. Since the purpose of the financial plan is to provide you with some measure of emotional as well as financial security, it is important to define your limits and objectives in this area as clearly as possible. Some of us are willing to take major gambles; others would rather earn minimal rates of return rather than take even the smallest chance. Being a gambler or a cautious investor doesn't make us right or wrong; it simple makes us human. All of us have our own tolerances for risk, and that tolerance level must be established and respected by the planner. By the end of this session, your planner should have all of the data necessary to begin to work on your plan.

Analysis of Your Needs and Objectives

The first thing a planner should do with all of the information you have provided is to determine the extent to which your goals are currently being met and the likelihood of their long-term achievement if you were to continue to follow your present financial course.

Usually the facts and figures are fed into a computer to create a comparative picture between the actual and the ideal. The planner is then able to pinpoint the specific strengths and weaknesses of your current plan. In some instances it will be discovered that you are doing less than necessary (often in the areas of tax, investment, or estate planning) while in other cases you may be doing far more than is actually required (e.g., in the area of insurance and risk management) for the achievement of your goals.

Development of the Plan

The planner's next step should be to develop a comprehensive personal financial plan by building on existing strengths and correcting apparent weaknesses. It is at this stage that additional expertise is often called in to determine which of the many available alternatives would be most appropriate given your specific circumstances.

The plan is then developed and presented to the panel of experts for final review, recommendations, and revision. Once the team is satisfied, the plan is then produced for presentation to the client.

Presentation of the Plan

Ideally, the presentation of your personal financial plan should consist of a two-part process. First, the plan should be sent to you by mail or by courier for your personal review. Second, a meeting should be scheduled with the planner two or three weeks later to discuss the plan in detail.

As you read through the plan you have received, you should make a list of any questions you have for discussion at that meeting. Remember, it is *your* plan. If you are not happy with the recommendations of the planner, then alternatives must be found. The plan may need to be revised several times before you are thoroughly satisfied, and a good planner should be willing to spend whatever time is required to answer all of your questions in detail and to make any necessary revisions before you enter the next important part of the process.

Do not be afraid to challenge the planner. You have the right to ask why certain forms of insurance are being recommended or why specific investments are being suggested. Whatever you need to ask in order to be absolutely certain that the plan before you is the one you should be following, ask it.

Implementation of the Plan

As human beings we all seem to share a natural tendency to procrastinate. Even when we know we should be doing something that is in our own best interests, we tend to let it slide. We all agree that an annual medical check-up would be a good idea or that seeing our dentist every six months would be the wisest course of action, but how many of us actually follow through on our intentions? Unfortunately, very few.

Just as there are certain things we must do to maintain good physical health, there are specific things we must do to ensure our financial well-being. There are policies to be purchased, investments to be made, funds to be deposited on a regular basis, wills to be drawn up, trust funds to be established, and so forth. In the final analysis, the personal financial plan you have just been given is totally worthless unless you actually take the necessary steps to implement the recommendations of the plan. The retirement funds we need or the protection we want for our family won't be there tomorrow unless we take the necessary steps today. Agreeing that the recommendations of the plan make good sense is one thing; actually implementing those recommendations is another thing altogether. For the plan to succeed, agreement must be followed by action.

A good planner should be willing to work with you to see that all of the recommendations in the plan are implemented in a timely and acceptable manner; however, the ultimate responsibility for the success or the failure of the plan lies in your own hands at this point. Your planner can recommend a good estate attorney for updating your current will. The planner can even go so far as to make an appointment with this individual on your behalf; however, attending the appointment and making sure that all of the changes to your will are made in accordance with your personal financial plan are your responsibilities.

Periodic Review

Since financial plans are designed around human circumstances, they are necessarily subject to change. The birth of a new child, the death of an elderly parent, a change in employment status, a change in tax laws, or even a change in attitude are just a few of the reasons why your personal financial plan may need to be reviewed and modified.

At the very least, your financial planner should review your plan on an annual basis. Even though there have been no major changes in your financial condition over the past 12 months, a little fine tuning and a few adjustments may be in order. Since the financial plan is based on projected market trends, investment returns, and inflation rates, it is impossible for any planner to be 100 percent accurate about how things are going to be for you two or three years down the road. A certain number of unknowns are inevitable; and while these minor deviations may seem to be unimportant in the short-term scheme of things, over the long haul they may cause you to completely miss the mark. The only sure way to keep your personal finances firmly on track is to review your plan on an annual basis.

YOUR ROLE IN THE PROCESS

So far we have presented you with a general overview of what personal financial planning entails so that you will be able to select a competent planner as well as monitor his or her activities throughout the process. Now it is time to turn our attention to the specifics of the plan itself.

Part 2
Gathering the Facts: The Dollars and Sense

4
Your Current Net Worth

EFFECTING THE OUTCOME

Gathering the financial data upon which to build your financial future may be a tedious and time-consuming process, but it is critical to the success of your plan. As Aldous Huxley wisely observed, "Facts do not cease to exist because they are ignored." The withholding of any details, whether by intent or through carelessness, can have a disastrous effect on the overall outcome of the process.

The questions you will be asked in the following chapters are typical of the scope and nature of the information a financial planner will require in order to develop your personal plan. Hopefully, by taking the time to assemble all of this important information now, you will be well prepared to provide the facts the planner will need to create a comprehensive picture of your financial condition. At the very least, by completing these questionnaires and other related exercises in this book, you will have a more thorough understanding of your current circumstances.

Exercise 4–1
Personal Financial Planning Questionnaire—Part I

Personal Information

Your Name ______________________________

Spouse's Name ______________________________

Address ______________________________

____

Telephone: Home ______________ Office ______________

Date of Birth: Husband ______________ Wife ______________

Your Employer ______________________________

Your Occupation/Title ______________________________

Spouse's Employer ______________________________

Spouse's Occupation/Title ______________________________

Dependents (Children, elderly relations, other)

Name	Relationship	Date of Birth

RECOMMENDATIONS

As you can see in Exercise 4–1, the first portion of the financial planning questionnaire is simply a list of all of the basic facts and information about your family. However, there may be additional information the questionnaire does not address specifically, but which is highly relevant to your financial plan. For example, if one of your children is handicapped and requires special care, this fact should be brought to the attention of the planner. Other significant facts might include:

1. Previous marriages for either spouse
2. Children who are adopted or from previous marriages
3. Life expectancy of elderly relations for whom you are currently providing support
4. Possibilities of future inheritance
5. Proposed changes in career or employment status
6. Possibilities of divorce/marriage

Remember, all the information you provide to your planner will be handled in a highly professional and confidential manner. If there are personal factors that may affect your financial circumstances in the next few years, these matters should be brought to the attention of the planner.

RECOMMENDATIONS

If you do not have a financial advisor in each of the areas in Part II, Exercise 4–2, you should give strong consideration to lining up the ones you are lacking, even if you do not need their services right away. The best time to look for competent advisors is when you are not under the gun to get something done. The pressure of immediate need often forces us to rely on the services of

Exercise 4–2
Personal Financial Planning Questionnaire—Part II

Current Financial Advisors

Advisor	Name / Title	Firm / Address	Telephone
Accountant			
Attorney			
Banker			
Insurance Agent (Auto)			
Insurance Agent (Business)			
Insurance Agent (Disability)			
Insurance Agent (Home)			
Insurance Agent (Life)			
Insurance Agent (Medical)			
Investment Advisor			
Stockbroker			
Tax Advisor			
Trust Officer			

someone we would not work with if we had the time to make another choice.

By investigating the possibilities carefully, you may also be able to find financial advisors who can fulfill dual functions. For example, some public accountants specialize in tax matters while many family attorneys also have expertise in estate planning or fiduciary responsibilities. However, you should be careful to avoid putting all of your financial trust into the hands of one individual, even your financial planner. The old adage, "A jack of all trades and master of none" also applies to financial advisors.

When selecting a financial advisor, remember to look beyond his or her professional qualifications and educational background. Expertise is certainly important, but the personality of the advisor should be given equal consideration.

One of the advisor relationships most families overlook is with a local banker. Developing a good working relationship with a bank manager can make a world of difference to your financial affairs. He or she can provide excellent advice on a variety of issues including pension plans, investment alternatives, and trust funds. A bank manager can also be a valuable credit or personal reference, and can grant loan approval in circumstances that might otherwise be impossible. If you have not already done so, make an appointment and introduce yourself to your bank manager to open the lines of communication. Be sure to bring copies of personal tax returns and financial statements to the meeting to be kept in your bank file for future reference.

YOUR CURRENT NET WORTH

Net worth is determined by subtracting the total of all your liabilities from the total of all your assets. Basically, it gives you a bottom line look at your current financial condition, and provides an excellent comparison for determining whether your financial condition is improving or deteriorating on an annual basis.

Assets

1. **Cash.** Your current cash holdings can be determined easily by counting all of the cash you have on hand at this moment in your pocket, your wallet, or your purse, and by asking the bank teller for a current balance on all of your accounts.
2. **Personal Loans/Accounts Receivable.** Any funds you have loaned to others and for which you anticipate eventual repayment should be listed here. Accounts receivable would include such things as holding a second mortgage on someone's home or an anticipated tax refund. Do not include any loans or accounts receivable for your business interests since these will be listed in another section.
3. **Investments.** Determining the current value of your investments is not really as difficult as you may think. Here are a few suggestions to simplify the task:
   a. **Stocks, Bonds, Mutual Funds.** The current value of these investments can be found in the financial section of your daily newspaper.
   b. **Government Bonds.** Refer to the current cash value given on the bond table.
   c. **Cash Value of Life Insurance.** Contact your life insurance agent for the current cash value of all policies.
   d. **Collectibles.** Your local librarian can help you find publications that list current values of collectibles such as coins, paintings, gems, antiques, and so forth. Also, check the Yellow Pages of your local telephone directory for businesses that deal in these items. Some merchants are willing to give estimated values of collectibles at no cost. A formal appraisal can cost as much as 10 percent of the items' value.
   e. **Limited Partnerships.** Your accountant or tax advisor can help you establish the current value of limited partnerships.

4. **Fixed Assets.** Fixed assets refer to those items that cannot be readily or easily converted into cash and that generally have a more prolonged lifespan.

   a. **Real Estate.** Having real estate professionally appraised can be expensive and is not really necessary unless you intend to refinance or seek a home equity loan within the next few months. A relatively accurate appraisal of the current market value of all real estate holdings can be obtained by researching classified ads and local real estate office circulars. Many real estate firms provide market analysis services at no cost to potential home-sellers.

   b. **Automobiles.** Your local library, used car dealer, bank, or credit union have current copies of the "blue book," which you can use to determine the value of your vehicles. Classified ads can also be a good way to determine current market values.

5. **Personal Property.** Personal property (household furnishings, clothing, etc.) should be listed in terms of its current market value (i.e., what you could sell it for) rather than what it would cost to replace those items at today's prices if they were lost or stolen.

6. **Pensions/Annuities.** Check with your bank, employer, and/or insurance agent for current values. You can also request an up-to-date total in your Social Security account from the Social Security office by completing a simple request card (Figure 4–1).

7. **Business Interests.**

   a. **Business Equity.** If you are self-employed, list the amount of equity you own in your business based on its current value (e.g., if your business is valued at $50,000 and you own 50 percent of the business you would write down $25,000). The easiest way to determine the approximate value of a small business is simply to subtract

Figure 4–1
Social Security Request Card

FOLD HERE

FOR SSA USE ONLY

AX

SP

REQUEST FOR STATEMENT OF EARNINGS
(PLEASE PRINT IN INK OR USE TYPEWRITER)

I REQUEST A SUMMARY STATEMENT OF EARNINGS FROM MY SOCIAL SECURITY RECORD

NH — Full name you use in work or business: First | Middle Initial | Last

SN — Social Security Number shown on your card

DB — Your date of birth: Month | Day | Year — A

MA — Other Social Security number(s) you have used

SX — Your Sex: ☐ Male ☐ Female

AK — Other name(s) you have used (Include your maiden name)

FOLD HERE

PRIVACY STATEMENT

The Social Security Administration (SSA) is authorized to collect information asked on this form under section 205 of the Social Security Act. It is needed so SSA can quickly identify your record and prepare the earnings statement you requested. While you are not required to furnish the information, failure to do so may prevent your request from being processed. The information will be used primarily for issuing your earnings statement.

I am the individual to whom the record pertains. I understand that if I knowingly and willingly request or receive a record about an individual under false pretenses I would be guilty of a Federal crime and could be fined up to $5000.

Sign your name here: (Do not print) | TELEPHONE NO (Area Code) | DATE

SEND THE STATEMENT TO: (to be completed in ALL cases.)

PN — Name

AD — Address (Number and Street, Apt. No., P.O. Box, or Rural Route)

City and State | ZP — Zip Code

Form SSA-7004-PC-OP2 (9/85)

all of the liabilities from all of the assets, including receivables.

b. **Company Profit-Sharing.** Your employer will be able to provide you with information on the current value of your shares in the company profit-sharing 410-K (cash savings), and stock-purchase plans.

Liabilities

1. **Unpaid Bills/Accounts Payable.** Include all outstanding amounts owed to your creditors. Where monthly payments are involved such as rent or insurance premiums, list only those payments that are due or past due at this time.
2. **Installment Loans.** List the amount needed to pay off the outstanding principal balance on each of these loans.
3. **Real Estate Loans/Mortgages.** List the outstanding principal balance for any real estate loans or mortgages. Your bank or mortgage holder will be able to give you the exact payoff balances.
4. **Credit Cards/Revolving Charge Accounts.** Refer to your most recent statements to determine the exact payoff balances.

RECOMMENDATIONS

One of the major objectives of personal financial planning is to increase your overall net worth by increasing the asset side of the balance sheet while simultaneously reducing the liabilities column. However, it should be remembered that the bottom line in Exercise 4–3 is not the only important figure on your financial statement. In fact, there are many equally important areas that should be given serious attention.

Liquidity

You may have a total net worth of several million dollars, but if those funds are all tied up in long-term mortgages or business equity you could still be in serious financial trouble if you had to come up with several thousand dollars on short notice.

Exercise 4–3
Personal Financial Planning Questionnaire—Part III

Current Net Worth

ASSETS

1. Cash
   a. On hand ________
   b. Savings Account ________
   c. Checking Account ________
   Total $ ____________

2. Personal Loans/Accounts Receivable
   a. Loans ________
   b. Accounts Receivable ________
   Total ____________

3. Investments
   a. Stocks ________
   b. Bonds ________
   c. Mutual Funds ________
   d. Government Securities ________
   e. Cash Value of Life Insurance ________
   f. Collectibles ________
   g. Limited Partnerships ________
   Total ____________

Subtotal $ ____________

Carry Forward Subtotal of Previous Page $ __________

4. Fixed Assets (market value)
   a. Personal Residence __________
   b. Vacation Property __________
   c. Rental Property __________
   d. Undeveloped Property __________
   e. Automobiles __________
   f. Other Vehicles __________
   Total __________

5. Personal Property (market value)
   a. Jewelry/Furs __________
   b. Household Furnishings __________
   c. Other Personal Property __________
   Total __________

6. Pensions/Annuities
   a. IRA __________
   b. Keogh/HR–10 __________
   c. Company (vested) __________
   d. Social Security __________
   e. Annuities (cash value) __________
   f. Other __________
   Total __________

Subtotal $ __________

(continued)

Exercise 4–3 continued

Carry Forward Subtotal of Previous Page $ ____________

7. Business Interests
   a. Business Equity __________
   b. Company Profit-Sharing, Cash Savings and Stock Purchase Plans __________
   Total ____________

Total Assets $ ____________

LIABILITIES

1. Unpaid Bills/Accounts Payable
   a. Charge Accounts __________
   b. Credit Cards __________
   c. Utilities __________
   d. Personal Loans __________
   e. Rent __________
   f. Loans on Life Insurance __________
   g. Federal Taxes __________
   h. State Taxes __________
   i. Local/Property Taxes __________
   j. Insurance Premiums __________
   k. Other __________
   Total $ ____________

Subtotal $ ____________

Carry Forward Subtotal of Previous Page $ ________

2. Installment Loans (current balance)

   a. Automobile ________
   b. Other Vehicles ________
   c. Education ________
   d. Other ________

   Total ________

3. Real Estate Loans/Mortgages (current balances)

   a. Personal Residence ________
   b. Vacation Property ________
   c. Rental Property ________
   d. Undeveloped Property ________
   e. Other ________

   Total ________

Total Liabilities $ ________

Current Net Worth = **ASSETS** – **LIABILITIES**

= $ ________ – $ ________

= $ ________

It is recommended that you have the equivalent of at least six months' fixed and variable expenses available in cash or highly liquid investments to cover yourself in the event of emergency situations. For example, if your monthly living expenses are $2000, you should have at least $12,000 set aside in either your savings account or in investments that could be converted quickly into cash. Exercise 4-4 will help you to determine the extent of your liquidity.

Exercise 4–4
Your Personal Liquidity Status

Total Monthly Expenses	$________
Liquidity Requirements (Monthly expenses X 6)	$________
LiquidAssets	$________
Total Cash Assets	$________
Total Liquid Investments	$________
Total Liquid Assets	$________
Total Liquid Assets – Liquidity Requirements	$________

If your answer is on the plus side, you have sufficient liquid assets for emergency or unexpected opportunity situations. If your answer indicates a negative balance, then whatever your current net worth may be, some adjustments should be made to increase your overall liquidity.

Investment of Surplus Funds

A good financial statement is a balanced statement. While it is important to have sufficient liquidity, it is equally important not to be excessively liquid. In other words, you do not want to have an excess of surplus funds sitting idly in the bank drawing minimal interest. If your total liquid assets (especially those in checking and savings accounts) are in excess of your liquidity requirements, then it is important to find a more profitable resting place for those idle funds.

One of the worst offenders on the list of places where idle cash tends to accumulate is the personal checking account. Week after week we deposit our hard-earned money into these accounts and get little or nothing in return for our diligence other than the promise of free checkwriting privileges or an interest rate so low it barely flickers on the financial scale.

Most banks now offer some form of money-market account that provides an attractive interest rate in exchange for limited checkwriting privileges. Generally, you are allowed to write only three checks per month on such accounts without penalty. However, you are usually free to make an unlimited number of cash withdrawals. By depositing your paycheck and temporary surplus funds into one of these accounts and then transferring only the amount you need to cover the checks you have written or will be writing over the next three to five days on your zero or low-interest checking account, you can make your hard-earned dollars work harder for you.

At first glance, this may seem like a lot of extra work for very little reward. For example, $2000 in a money-market account earning 6 percent per annum only amounts to 10 dollars a month, which is approximately equivalent to 33 cents a day. But as the saying goes, "If you learn to take care of the pennies, the dollars will take care of themselves." As Table 4–1 indicates, those few pennies a day can add up to a considerable sum over a human lifetime.

Table 4–1
Interest Earned on $2,000 Invested at 6 percent per annum

Number of Years	Interest Earned
1 year	$ 120.00
5 years	676.45
10 years	1581.70
15 years	2793.12
20 years	4414.27
25 years	6583.74
30 years	9486.98

Solvency

Solvency refers to the extent to which your total assets exceed (hopefully) your total liabilities. Solvency can be determined by dividing your total liabilities by your total assets (Exercise 4–5). The lower the figure, the more solvent you are.

Exercise 4–5
Your Solvency Percentage

Example:

Total Liabilities	$154,000
Total Assets	$362,000
Total Liabilities ÷ Total Assets =	.43
Total Liabilities	$ ______
Total Assets	$ ______
Total Liabilities ÷ Total Assets =	$ ______

If your solvency factor is 1 or higher, then the first order of business must be to focus on the reduction of debt. If the factor is .1 or lower, it is possible that you are not making sufficient use of leverage to increase your assets and overall net worth.

Your Working Net Worth

Working net worth is the total of all *productive* assets (i.e., assets that are, or have the capability of, producing income) less any liabilities pertaining to those assets (Exercise 4–6). This bottom

Exercise 4–6
Your Working Net Worth

Example:

Total Assets	$524,375
– Equity in Personal Residence	(146,000)
– Equity in Vacation Property	(43,150)
– Value of Automobiles and Other Vehicles	(20,225)
Total Productive Assets	$315,000
Total Liabilities	$256,000
– Mortgage on Personal Residence	(80,000)
– Mortgage on Vacation Property	(10,000)
– Outstanding Loans on Automobiles and Other Vehicles	(8,000)
Total Productive Liabilities	$158,000
Total Working Net Worth	$157,000
Percentage of Total Net Worth	30%

Total Assets	$ ________
– Total Nonproductive Assets	(________)
Total Working Assets	$ ________
Total Liabilities	$ ________
– Total Nonproductive Liabilities	(________)
Total Productive Liabilities	$ ________
Total Working Net Worth	$ ________
Total Percentage of Net Worth	________%

line figure provides you with the actual amount you have to work with or invest to increase your overall net worth.

Obviously, the more funds you have to work with, the more quickly you can improve your financial condition. Throughout this book we will be examining the various ways in which you can increase your total working net worth and consequently, improve your financial condition through personal financial planning. For the moment, however, you should be aware of the five basic methods that are available to increase your working net worth:

Create more working capital by reducing current living expenses

Create more working capital by reducing current tax liability

Create more working capital by increasing return on productive assets

Create more working capital by decreasing liabilities

Create more working capital by converting non-productive assets into productive assets

NEXT STEPS

Before we continue with the next part of the personal financial planning questionnaire, it is important to capture in writing (in Exercise 4–7) your general observations so far. These observations will form the framework for your discussions with your financial planner as well as the foundation upon which you will develop your personal financial planning goals.

Exercise 4-7
Personal Financial Planning Questionnaire Summary—Parts I–III

1. **Part I: Personal Information**

   a. Additional personal information the planner will need to know:

   ____

   ____

   ____

2. **Part II: Your Current Financial Advisors**

   a. Financial advisors whose services are unsatisfactory

   ____

   ____

   ____

   b. Financial advisors with whom I need to establish a working relationship to round out my personal financial advisory committee

   ____

   ____

   ____

3. **Part III: Your Current Net Worth**

   a. Assets $ ________

   ____

   ____

   ____

(continued)

Exercise 4–7 continued

b. Liabilities $ ________

____

____

____

c. Current net worth $ ________

____

____

____

d. Liquidity requirements $ ________

Current surplus/deficit (±) $ ________

____

____

____

e. Investment of surplus funds

Funds in low/zero-interest accounts $ ________

____

____

____

f. Solvency factor

____

____

____

g. Your current working net worth $ ________

Percentage of current net worth ______ %

____

____

____

5
Analysis of Your Current Assets

DESCRIPTION OF FIXED ASSETS

The purpose of this section of the questionnaire (Exercise 5–1) is to provide more information about the fixed assets you and your family currently own.

1. **Asset.** List the asset held and provide a brief description if necessary (e.g., vacation property, 3-bedroom, lakefront cottage).
2. **Owner(s).** Who are the owners of the asset? Husband only? Wife only? Husband and wife? Husband and parents? What percentage of the asset does each of the owners hold?
3. **Title.** How is title to the asset held? Tenants in common? Joint ownership?
4. **Reason(s) For Holding Asset.** Family vacations? Tax deductible expense? Long-term appreciation?
5. **Anticipated Changes.** Do you intend to sell the property in the next few years? Will there be any changes in ownership? Do you intend to refinance the asset?

Exercise 5–1
Personal Financial Planning Questionnaire—Part IV

Description of Fixed Assets

Asset ____________________
Owner(s) ____________________ ______%
& Percentage ____________________ ______%
of Ownership ____________________ ______%
How Is Title Held? ____________________
Reason for Holding Asset ____________________
____
Anticipated Changes ____________________
____

Asset ____________________
Owner(s) ____________________ ______%
& Percentage ____________________ ______%
of Ownership ____________________ ______%
How Is Title Held? ____________________
Reason for Holding Asset ____________________
____
Anticipated Changes ____________________
____

Asset ____________________
Owner(s) ____________________ ______%
& Percentage ____________________ ______%
of Ownership ____________________ ______%
How Is Title Held? ____________________
Reason for Holding Asset ____________________
____
Anticipated Changes ____________________
____

Exercise 5–1 continued

Asset ____
Owner(s) ____________________________ ______ %
& Percentage _________________________ ______ %
of Ownership _________________________ ______ %
How Is Title Held? ________________________________
Reason for Holding Asset ____________________________
____
Anticipated Changes ________________________________
____

Asset ____
Owner(s) ____________________________ ______ %
& Percentage _________________________ ______ %
of Ownership _________________________ ______ %
How Is Title Held? ________________________________
Reason for Holding Asset ____________________________
____
Anticipated Changes ________________________________
____

Asset ____
Owner(s) ____________________________ ______ %
& Percentage _________________________ ______ %
of Ownership _________________________ ______ %
How Is Title Held? ________________________________
Reason for Holding Asset ____________________________
____
Anticipated Changes ________________________________
____

RECOMMENDATIONS

Ownership Titles

How assets are held may seem unimportant at the moment, but ownership titles make a considerable difference in the event of an unexpected death or change in marital status. The following are the most common forms of title holding or ownership.

Joint Tenancy with Right of Survivorship

Co-owners may dispose of their share of the property without having to obtain the consent of the other. In other words, if you and your spouse were equal partners in the ownership of a vacation property and one of you elected to sell his or her share, the sale could be made by one spouse without obtaining the consent of the other. The right of survivorship clause guarantees that in the event of death all ownership would be transferred automatically to the surviving owner or owners.

This form of ownership can also apply to bank accounts that are jointly held. The only difference (and it can be a significant one in the event of an unstable marriage) is that either party may have access to the entire balance in the account, not just his or her share.

Because the right of survivorship clause automatically guarantees that the survivor will inherit all funds in the jointly held account, it is important for estate tax purposes to keep accurate records of all deposits and/or withdrawals made by both contributors. Otherwise, the person who is the major contributor to the account could find him or herself paying inheritance taxes on funds that were actually his or her own in the first place.

Tenancy By Entirety

With this method of ownership neither spouse may dispose of his or her share of the property without the legal consent of the other.

All ownership would be transferred automatically to the surviving spouse in the event of death.

Tenants In Common

This form of ownership is similar to joint tenancy in that co-owners may dispose of their share of the property without requiring the legal consent of the other owner(s). However, unlike joint tenancy, the surviving owner is not automatically entitled to the share that was owned by the deceased. Instead, the deceased owner's share will be transferred to his or her estate for disposition.

Outright Ownership

This refers to property that is owned entirely by one individual. Unless otherwise stated by a binding legal agreement such as a marital contract, divorce agreement, or community property laws, all personal property purchased by an individual during his or her lifetime is automatically considered to be his or her sole property and will become a part of his or her estate at death. Personal property can include personal effects such as jewelry, clothing, and furniture as well as certain assets such as real estate, stocks, bonds, bank accounts, and so forth.

Community Property

In states where community property laws apply, spouses may own both personal and community property. Generally, personal property consists of all assets and personal effects owned by the spouse at the time of marriage as well as any property that is obtained by inheritance during the marriage.

Community property refers to any property or assets acquired during the marriage by either or both spouses unless a specific legal document exists to assign the property to another form of ownership. Although the laws regarding management of community property vary from state to state, the laws governing disposition generally allow the spouse to dispose of his or her half of all community property by stipulating such personal wishes in a legal will or an operation of law such as a trust.

Community property is a very complex issue and can affect the assets and liabilities of a spouse not only in the state in which he or she is currently residing, but also in the states where the couple did or will reside. For example, property owned by a couple in a community property state may still be considered community property even if they relocate to a common law state. Conversely, property owned by the couple in a common law state may not be declared community property if the couple were to move to a community property state. Because of the complexity of community property laws, it is important to obtain legal advice on the issue of property ownership from a competent estate attorney or another similarly qualified expert.

Present and Future Interests

This form of ownership is particularly useful for transferring assets through several generations of ownership. Suppose you wanted your surviving spouse to benefit from the income in a trust fund for his or her remaining years, however, you didn't want your irresponsible son to inherit the remainder of that trust at the death of your spouse. By assigning your spouse the "present" interest, he or she would be entitled to the income from the trust for the balance of his or her life. Then, by assigning the "future" interest (i.e., whatever funds remain in the trust) to your favorite nephew, your assets would pass to the heirs of your choice rather than the heirs of your spouse's choice.

Legal and Equitable Interests

This form of title holding grants to a trustee or fiduciary the legal ownership of your property. The trustee or fiduciary has the responsibility of managing your property for the beneficiaries of that trust. As a result, the "legal" interest is granted to the managers of the trust while the "equitable" interest (i.e., the income from the trust) is granted to the beneficiaries. This method can be particularly useful when minor children are likely to become the beneficiaries or when the surviving spouse might lack the financial acumen to effectively manage the decedent's estate.

As you can see, there are a number of ways in which property can be held, each with its own distinct advantages and drawbacks. Understanding each of the alternatives and giving careful consideration to the way in which all of your assets should be held can make a major difference in the years ahead.

Percentage of Total Assets

It is important to determine the percentage each asset represents of your current net worth to give you a better sense of the extent to which your past, present, and future earnings are being invested in nonproductive (i.e., non-income-producing) assets.

To determine the percentage of each asset, in Exercise 5–2 multiply the value of the asset by 100 and then divide the figure by your current net worth.

Example:

Current Net Worth	$350,000
Value of Personal Residence	150,000
$150,000 X 100 = $15,000,000 ÷ $350,000 =	42.86%

Exercise 5–2
Asset-to-Net Worth Percentage

Your Current Net Worth	$__________
1. ____________________	__________%
2. ____________________	__________%
3. ____________________	__________%
4. ____________________	__________%
5. ____________________	__________%
6. ____________________	__________%
Total Percentage of All Fixed Assets	__________%

Burden of Liability

The purpose of Exercise 5–3 is to determine the burden of liability each of your fixed assets places on you. In order to calculate the burden of each asset, multiply the outstanding liability of each asset by 100 and divide that sum by your current net worth.

Example:

Current Net Worth	$350,000
Mortgage on Personal Residence	100,000
$100,000 X 100 = $10,000,000 ÷ $350,000 =	28.57%

Exercise 5–3
Liability-to-Net Worth Percentage

Your Current Net Worth	$________
1. ________________	________%
2. ________________	________%
3. ________________	________%
4. ________________	________%
5. ________________	________%
6. ________________	________%
Total Percentage of All Fixed Assets	________%

After completing this exercise, you may find that the value certain assets bring to your financial condition is far outweighed by the liabilities they carry. In the examples given for these two exercises we see that while this individual's personal residence increases the asset side of his personal net worth by 42.86 percent, it also decreases his net worth by carrying with it a liability equal to 28.57 percent. By subtracting these two figures (42.86 – 28.57) we could say that, in essence, his current personal residence is increasing his current net worth by only 14.29%.

By itself, this particular figure has very little significance. However, in the next chapter, when we take a look at the percentage of current income that is being used to hold onto this asset, we begin to understand why it may be highly advantageous to consider selling or exchanging some of our current fixed assets in order to enhance both our current investment-earning capacity and our overall financial condition. If 75 percent of your current income is being used to hold onto assets that offer no investment value and that increase your net worth by less than 15 percent, obviously some adjustments should be made. For the moment, however, we merely want to ascertain the overall impact each of our fixed assets has on our net worth by subtracting (in Exercise 5–4) the liability percentage from the asset percentage.

Exercise 5–4
Impact of Fixed Assets on Net Worth

Your Fixed Assets	Overall Impact
1. ____________________	__________%
2. ____________________	__________%
3. ____________________	__________%
4. ____________________	__________%
5. ____________________	__________%
6. ____________________	__________%

DESCRIPTION OF INVESTMENTS

In order to develop your plan, specific information about all of your current investments will be required. Your stockbroker and/or investment advisors can help you develop a complete listing of all of your current investment holdings.

1. **Description.** List the type of investment and a brief description of the investment (e.g., IBM/100 Shares).
2. **Year Acquired.** When was the investment purchased?
3. **Cost Basis.** What was the amount you originally paid for this investment?
4. **Current Value.** What is the current market value of this investment assuming you were to sell it today?
5. **Annual Income.** How much income did you earn on this investment last year (before taxes)? If the investment was held solely for tax credits or deductions, list the tax dollars you saved. If you have held the investment for less than a year, determine the average monthly rate of return and multiply that amount by 12.
6. **Percentage of Total Portfolio.** This section (Exercise 5–5) should be completed after reading the following section entitled "Diversification of Your Investment Portfolio."

Exercise 5–5
Asset Value to Total Portfolio Percentage

Description	Year Acq'd	Cost Basis	Current Value	Annual Income	% of Total

RECOMMENDATIONS

Diversification of Your Investment Portfolio

One of the first aspects of your investment portfolio that the planner will want to examine is the degree of diversification it represents. Far too often people make the mistake of investing all of their eggs in one basket. This form of investing generally results in lower overall returns. Moreover, it also exposes the investor to considerable risk in the event of a drastic change in market conditions affecting that investment. People who invested solely in real estate in the past are well aware of the consequences of that foolish action. Many have lost considerable amounts of money due to changes in property appreciation, laws governing rental units, and, more recently, tax laws affecting methods of depreciation and permissible write-offs. By the same token, those who have invested solely in stocks have had their share of significant losses when the market unexpectedly plummets several hundred points as it did on October 19, 1987—an event that has subsequently (and appropriately) been referred to as "Black Monday."

The only truly effective way to safeguard against the unexpected and to capitalize on current and future earning rates is to be certain that your investment portfolio is well diversified by spreading your investment dollars over several areas rather than focusing them all in one or two sectors. The purpose of this exercise, then, is to determine exactly where you are currently investing your money, and the extent to which your current portfolio is well diversified, by calculating the percentage of each of your productive assets.

First, multiply the current value of each asset by 100 and divide that sum by your total working net worth. Then write that percentage in the last column in Exercise 5–5.

Once you have established the percentage value of each of your current productive assets, the next step is to use those percentages to determine the overall composition of your portfo-

Exercise 5–6
Overall Composition of Portfolio

Type of Asset		Percentage
Business Interests	1. Own Company	
	2. Interest in Other Companies	
	Total Business Investments	
Fixed Income	1. Money Market (Certificates of Deposits, T-bills, etc.)	
	2. Bonds	
	Total Fixed Income Investments	
Stocks	1. Growth Stocks (Future Value)	
	2. Income Stocks (Current Income)	
	3. Mutual Funds	
	Total Stock Investments	
Real Estate	1. Limited Partnerships	
	2. Rental Property	
	3. Undeveloped Property	
	Total Real Estate Investments	
Speculation	1. Futures Contracts/Options	
	2. Gas/Oil	
	3. Gold/Precious Metals	
	Total Speculation Investments	
Collectibles		
Other		

lio (Exercise 5–6). For example, by adding up the various percentages in each of the categories listed in this exercise you may find that 57 percent of your portfolio is in stocks while the other 43 percent is in collectibles. A quick glance at these figures will help you to determine whether or not your portfolio is adequately diversified or excessively concentrated.

Objectives of Portfolio

In addition to studying the composition of your current portfolio, the planner will also study its overall objectives. Basically, the purpose of an investment portfolio is to achieve one or more of the goals listed in Exercise 5–7.

Exercise 5–7
Priority of Investment Objectives

______	______	Insure safety of principal
______	______	Provide additional source of current income
______	______	Provide additional current income to meet specific needs (e.g., purchasing a home)
______	______	Provide additional future income to meet specific needs (e.g., child's education)
______	______	Provide future income for retirement
______	______	Hedge against inflation
______	______	Provide a source of contingency funds through emphasis on liquidity
______	______	Minimize current tax consequences
______	______	Minimize future tax consequences
______	______	Increase value of estate for heirs

In the space provided in the first column in Exercise 5–7, rank each of these investment objectives in their order of importance to you, with 1 being the most important and 10 being the least important.

When you have completed this, review the percentages you assigned to each of your invested assets in Exercise 5–6. Starting with the assets that have the highest percentage, determine which of the investment objectives these assets are currently meeting. For example, if the greatest percentage of your assets lies in limited partnerships and gas and oil ventures, the emphasis of your current portfolio is probably on minimizing current tax consequences. You would therefore write a "1" in the appropriate space in the second column. If the next greatest percentage of your assets lies in growth stocks and collectibles (investments which will provide future rather than current financial gains) you would write a "2" in the appropriate space beside the objective these investments are most likely to meet. Finally, compare the two sets of figures in order to determine how well your current investment program is meeting your investment objectives.

The purpose of this exercise is to provide you with a point of comparison between your goals and your current investment program. If your primary personal objective is to create current income while maintaining safety of principal, and the bulk of your investment portfolio is in speculative ventures and long-term growth stocks, then obviously some adjustments must be made.

NEXT STEPS

Before we move on to the final section of the financial planning questionnaire, be sure to capture your observations regarding your current assets in writing in Exercise 5–8.

Exercise 5-8
Personal Financial Planning Questionnaire—Summary
Part IV

A. Fixed Assets

1. Changes in ownership titles to be considered

2. Fixed assets that could be converted to productive assets

B. Productive Assets

1. Assets that could be converted to increase income or diversification of portfolio

2. Assets that are not consistent with current investment objectives

6
Projected Sources and Uses of Funds

The purpose of this section of the questionnaire is to estimate your family's monthly income and expenditures in order to determine surplus funds that will be available for investment.

SOURCES OF FUNDS

In Exercise 6–1, estimate your projected monthly income for this year. When specific information is not available, estimate earnings based on last year's income. To determine monthly income from nonmonthly sources (e.g., bonuses, refunds, dividends, etc.) calculate the estimated annual earnings and divide that figure by 12.

USES OF FUNDS

In Exercise 6–2, estimate your projected monthly expenses for this year. When specific information is not available, determine your annual expenses by referring to your checkbook and credit card receipts for three to six months and dividing that total by the appropriate figure to obtain a monthly average.

Exercise 6–1
Personal Financial Planning Questionnaire—Part V

SOURCES OF FUNDS

1. Salary
   a. Husband ________
   b. Wife ________
2. Bonuses/Commissions/Employer Contributions to Pension, Thrift, or Profit-Sharing Plan
   a. Husband ________
   b. Wife ________
3. Taxable and Nontaxable Interest
   a. Savings Accounts ________
   b. Personal Loans ________
   c. Taxable Investments ________
   d. Nontaxable Investments ________
   e. Pension Plans ________
4. Rents/Royalties ________
5. Tax Refunds
   a. Federal ________
   b. State/Local ________
6. Alimony/Child Support ________
7. Other ________

TOTAL SOURCES OF FUNDS $ ________

Exercise 6–2
Personal Financial Planning Questionnaire—Part VI

USES OF FUNDS

1. Taxes
   - a. Federal ________
   - b. State/Local ________
   - c. Property ________
   - Total $ ________
2. Employee Deductions for Federal and/or State Disability and/or Unemployment Programs
   - a. Federal ________
   - b. State ________
   - Total ________
3. Insurance Premiums
   - a. Homeowners ________
   - b. Vacation Property ________
   - c. Rental Property ________
   - d. Other Property ________
   - e. Medical/Dental ________
   - f. Automobile ________
   - g. Other Vehicles ________
   - h. Life Insurance ________
   - i. Disability ________
   - j. Liability ________
   - k. Business ________
   - Total ________

Subtotal $ ________

(continued)

Exercise 6–2 continued

Carry Forward Subtotal of Previous Page $ ____________

4. Mortgage Payments
   a. Residence ____________
   b. Vacation Property ____________
   c. Rental Property ____________
   d. Other ____________
   Total ____________

5. Housing Expenses
   a. Rent ____________
   b. Gas/Oil ____________
   c. Telephone ____________
   d. Electricity ____________
   e. Waste Removal ____________
   f. Water ____________
   g. Maintenance ____________
   h. Domestic Services ____________
   i. Improvements ____________
   j. Furnishings ____________
   Total ____________

6. Automobile Expenses
   a. Payments ____________
   b. Gas/Oil ____________
   c. Maintenance ____________
   d. Licenses ____________
   e. Parking/Tolls ____________
   Total ____________

Subtotal $ ____________

Carry Forward Subtotal of Previous Page $ ____________

7. Installment Loans/Credit Payments
   a. Personal __________
   b. Education __________
   c. Business __________
   d. Credit/Charge Cards __________
   e. Other __________
   Total ____________

8. Pensions/Investments/Savings
   a. IRA/Keogh/HR-10 __________
   b. Employee Pension __________
   c. Savings __________
   d. Mutual Funds __________
   e. Annuities __________
   f. Profit Sharing Plan __________
   g. Stocks/Bonds __________
   h. Securities __________
   i. Stock Options __________
   j. Safe Deposit Box __________
   k. Legal/Accounting __________
   l. Other __________
   Total ____________

Subtotal $ ____________

(continued)

Exercise 6–2 continued

Carry Forward Subtotal of Previous Page $ ____________

9. Family Living Expenses
   a. Groceries ____________
   b. Meals at Work/School ____________
   c. Clothing ____________
   d. Cleaning/Laundry ____________
   e. Gifts ____________
   f. Commuting ____________
   g. Tuition/Books ____________
   h. Personal Care ____________
   i. Pet Care ____________
   j. Daycare/Babysitters ____________
   k. Allowances ____________
   l. Miscellaneous ____________
   Total ____________

10. Nonreimbursed Medical/Dental Care
   a. Health Plan Fees ____________
   b. Medical Care ____________
   c. Dental Care ____________
   d. Medication/Drugs ____________
   e. Counsel/Therapy ____________
   f. Vision/Hearing ____________
   Total ____________

Subtotal $ ____________

Carry Forward Subtotal of Previous Page		$ ________
11. Recreation		
a. Membership/Dues	________	
b. Subscriptions/Books	________	
c. Records/Video/Games	________	
d. Entertainment	________	
e. Cable TV/Movies	________	
f. Hobbies/Computer	________	
g. Travel/Vacation	________	
h. Theatre/Concerts	________	
i. Other	________	
Total		________
12. Contributions	________	________
13. Alimony/Child Support	________	________
14. Expenses for Rental Property/Royalty Income	________	________
15. Other	________	________
TOTAL USES OF FUNDS		$ ________

Monthly Surplus/Deficit:

Total Sources of Funds		$ ________
Less Total Uses of Funds	–	$ ________
Monthly Surplus/Deficit		$ ________

THE BOTTOM LINE

Personal financial planning cannot, in and of itself, pave the way to fortune. It can only eliminate some of the unnecessary detours we might take or reduce the number of pitfalls we may encounter along the way. It should be remembered at all times that your future financial security will depend primarily on the raw materials you give your financial planner to work with.

As indicated by Table 6–1, there are three things in particular that will affect your financial condition over the long term:

1. The number of years available to you to increase your net worth
2. The rate of return on your investments
3. The amount you choose to invest

In most cases, the number of years we have to increase our total net worth will be limited by the number of earning years remaining to us. That is why the sooner we begin to take personal financial planning seriously, the better off we will be in a much shorter period of time. Not taking steps now to improve our financial condition means that we will be required to make severe cutbacks in the future.

As Table 6–1 also indicates, the rate of return on your investments can make a dramatic difference in the annual sum you will need to invest. Remember, however, that this chart reflects *gross* (i.e., pretax) earnings on your investment. That is why an important part of financial planning is the reduction of personal income tax. If, for example, you are in the 40 percent bracket, the gross return on your investment would be significantly lower. Finally, and most important of all, the extent to which your net worth increases over the years will in large part be determined by the funds that you are able to invest in your future.

Since the primary objective of personal financial planning is to make your available resources work as hard for you as you have

Table 6–1
Approximate Annual Investment Required to Accrue $500,000

Rate of Return	Number of Years Required							
	5	10	15	20	25	30	35	40
5%	86,180	37,860	22,070	14,400	9,830	7,165	5,270	3,940
6%	83,680	35,785	20,265	12,825	8,600	5,965	4,235	3,050
7%	81,270	33,820	18,595	11,400	7,390	4,945	3,280	2,340
8%	78,915	31,960	17,050	10,120	6,335	4,085	2,685	1,785
9%	76,660	30,195	15,625	8,965	5,415	3,365	2,215	1,360
10%	74,450	28,520	14,305	7,935	4,620	2,760	1,675	1,025
11%	72,335	26,940	13,090	7,015	3,935	2,2265	1,315	775
12%	70,275	25,440	11,975	6,195	3,350	1,850	1,030	580
13%	68,290	24,025	10,950	5,350	2,845	1,510	840	435
14%	66,350	22,680	10,005	4,820	2,410	1,230	630	325
15%	64,490	21,415	9,140	4,245	2,045	1,000	495	245

worked for them, it stands to reason that one of the pivotal points around which the plan will be developed is the funds that you make available to invest in your more affluent future. Notice, if you will, the way in which this last sentence was worded. We did not say the funds that "*are* available" but rather the funds that you "*make* available." And this is an important point for you to ponder. While it is not always possible to increase your current income, you can influence dramatically your monthly surplus funds any day you choose. No single expenditure is truly fixed. Everything from your mortgage payment to your tax payment can be changed by personal choice and financial strategy. Since the balance of this book is devoted primarily to financial strategy, we will focus our attention for the balance of this chapter on your current personal choices.

WHERE IT GOES

Writing down the dollars and cents is a good beginning for analyzing your monthly expenses. However, it doesn't really give you the total impact of your spending habits. The best way to accomplish this end is to convert the figures into percentages and the percentages into a graphic representation. First, determine the percentage of monthly income that you are currently allotting to each of the categories in Exercise 6–3 by multiplying the monthly expenditure by 100 and dividing that sum by your monthly income.

Exercise 6–3
Allocation of Monthly Income

Example:

Insurance Premiums	=	$ 1,000
$1,000 X 100	=	$100,000
Monthly Income	=	$ 5,000
Percentage ($100,000 ÷ $5,000)	=	20%

(continued)

Exercise 6–3 continued

Taxes	_____ %
Housing Expenses	_____ %
Food/Groceries	_____ %
Transportation	_____ %
Recreation/Vacation	_____ %
Health Care/Insurance	_____ %
Clothing	_____ %
Investments/Savings	_____ %
Contributions	_____ %
Other	_____ %

Once you have determined the percentage for each category, shade in that percentage on the graph in Exercise 6–4 to create a graphic representation of your monthly spending habits.

COMPARING YOUR SPENDING HABITS WITH OTHER AMERICAN FAMILIES

The graph in Figure 6–1 is based on the most recent statistics available from a variety of sources, including the U.S. Bureau of Labor Statistics, regarding the spending habits of the average four-person family whose annual gross income is approximately $40,000. Although your family situation and current income may be different, the overall picture presented on this chart will provide you with an interesting point of comparison concerning your own spending habits.

Exercise 6–4
Monthly Expenditures Graph

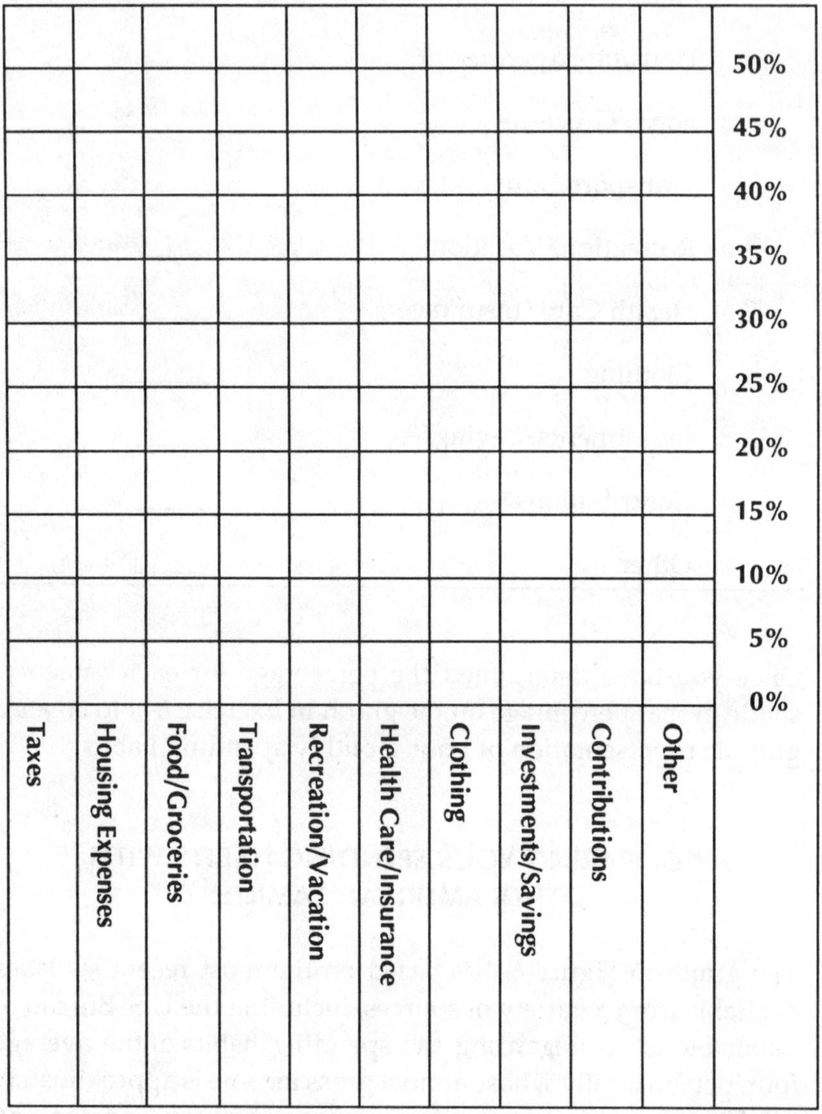

Figure 6–1
Monthly Expenditures for the Average American Family

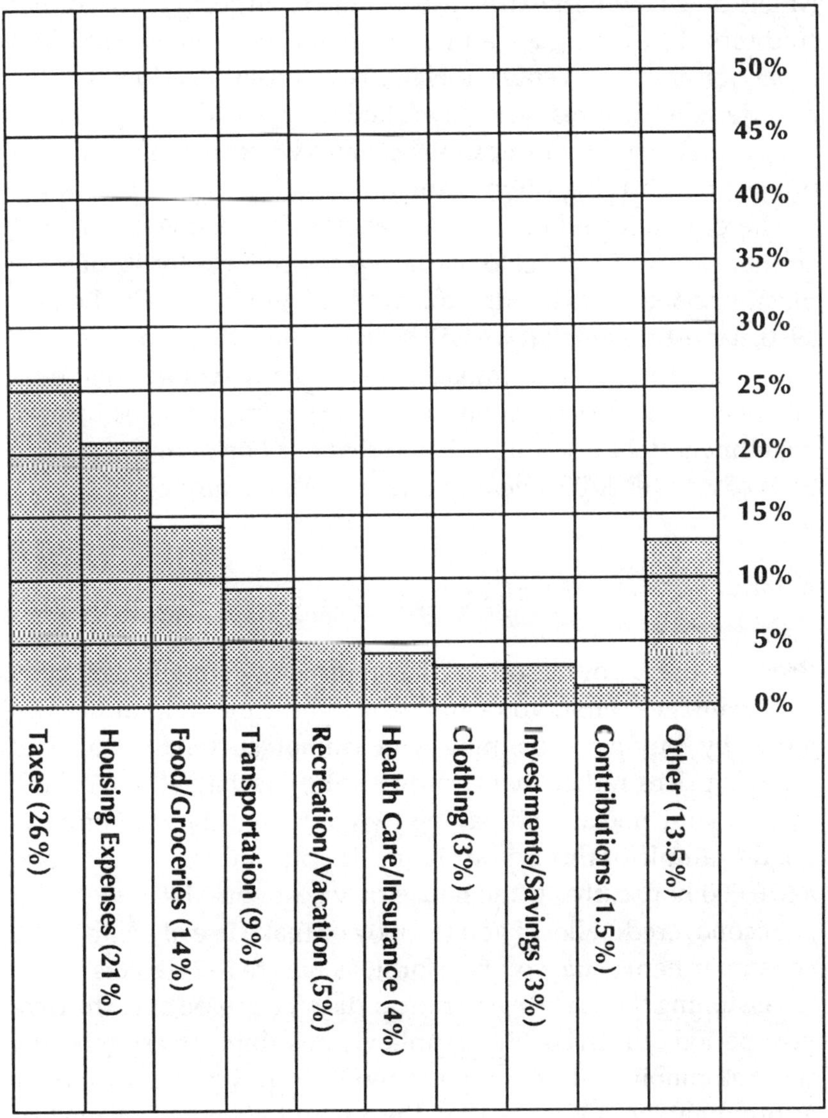

CREDIT ANALYSIS

Recent statistics indicate that nearly 18 percent of the average American's take-home (net) pay is already targeted for his or her creditors. With the ease and availability of so many different types of financial leverage, this figure has risen steadily over the past decade. As a result, many families now find themselves so deeply in debt that the question becomes whether they own their things or their things own them.

There is no question that Americans are in love with their credit cards. In fact, each of us carries approximately 4.2 of these plastic money cards in our wallets on any given day. By the year 1990, it is estimated that we will be using these cards for nearly $8 billion worth of annual transactions. Is it any wonder that over one half of the American population is paying off some form of installment debt every month and that our borrowing is costing each of us over $700 a year in interest charges alone?

The Uses of Credit

Properly used, your good credit can provide you with a number of advantages. First, you can use it to beat inflation at its own game by buying something you cannot currently afford at today's prices rather than waiting until you have the required cash in your pocket and paying two or three times the price. A good example of this is your home. If you wait ten years to buy a $70,000 house, that same house may cost you $140,000.

Second, credit allows you to enjoy or make use of a particular consumer item *while* you pay for it, as Figure 6–2 depicts.

Assuming the price tag on the car didn't increase over the two-year period (which is a highly unlikely possibility) by purchasing the automobile on credit your monthly payments would be approximately $130 more than the amount you would have had to save for the car, but you would be able to use the vehicle today rather than waiting another two years.

Figure 6–2
Purchasing a $13,000 Automobile

OPTION A:

Save $500 a month for 24 months at 9% interest
$500 × 24 × 9% = $13,000 (approximately)

OPTION B:

Take out a two-year $13,000 loan at 15% interest
$13,000 × 15% ÷ 24 = $630.33 monthly payment

Third, credit provides a perfect source of contingency or emergency funds to meet the unexpected. For example, if your car breaks down 200 miles from home and the mechanic wants $300 just to look under the hood, it is nice to know that a plastic card will compensate for the fact that you only have a $20 bill in your pocket.

Credit Abuse

Used wisely, credit can certainly be a valuable asset for most Americans. Unfortunately, it is just as easy to abuse as it is to use.

Surprisingly, it is not the poor who have a problem with credit management, but rather those in the middle- and upper-income brackets who slowly sign themselves into financial oblivion. Many find themselves spending a lifetime repaying the accumulated debts of a few years of overspending; an increasing number find bankruptcy to be the only practical solution for the excesses.

The real problem seems to arise when we use credit for purchasing life's luxuries rather than life's necessities. It is seldom the mortgage payment or the car payment or the business loan payment which sink us. Instead, it is the jewelry and furniture and clothing and vacations we sign for that ultimately lead us to financial disaster. Instead of saving for the extras, we sign for them, and therein lies the seeds of future financial misfortune.

Analyzing Your Credit Situation

Possession may be nine-tenths of the law, but it shouldn't be nine-tenths of your paycheck. According to most experts, the percentage of your disposable income (i.e., income after taxes) that is committed to some form of installment debt (not including your home mortgage) should never exceed 20 percent. A much safer policy by far is to keep your debt ratio in the 10 to 15 percent range.

To determine your current use or misuse of credit, refer to the fixed and variable expenses you listed in Exercise 6–2 and add up all monthly payments associated with personal loans, credit cards and other installment plans. Enter that total in Exercise 6–5, then divide your monthly net income (after taxes) by this figure to determine the percentage.

Exercise 6–5
Debt Ratio

Monthly Net Income	$	________
Total Fund Committed Each Month to Installment Debt	$	________
Percentage of Net Income	$	________

If the result is less than 10 percent, you are certainly to be congratulated for using your credit wisely. If you are in the 10-to-15 percent range, then you are still at an acceptable level of indebtedness, but you should exercise continued caution. If you are in the 15-to-20 percent range, then like most Americans, you are spending more than you earn on the luxuries you should be saving for or learning to live without for a few more years. Finally, if you are in the 20 percent and above range, you should either cut up your credit cards or seek professional credit counseling, or both. You are well on your way to either personal bankruptcy or financial chaos.

NEXT STEPS

Take a closer look at where your money is going every month and where these spending habits are leading you. In most cases, our spending habits are seldom compatible with our longer range goals; and for as long as we allow ourselves to spend freely today, these dreams will forever elude us.

7
A Plan for Your Life

Despite the fact that a financial plan consists primarily of dollars and cents, all of those numbers center around one primary objective: the achievement of your personal goals. Therefore, before your financial planner can present you with a comprehensive plan for your money, you must first present him or her with a concrete plan for your life.

For the most part, we human beings are so locked into the daily process of earning a living that we seldom, if ever, pause long enough to actually design a life. Instead, we seem to spend our childhood years imagining how it will one day be and our retirement years wondering how it all went wrong. Far too often a life that begins with untold hope and promise ends in bitter dillusionment and financial desperation simply because a dream was never given a plan to follow.

The reason most of us don't save more, invest more, and earn more is simply because we don't dream more and plan more. And since we have no future vision to guide our activities, we merely respond to the call of the here and now. Since we have no specific retirement goals, why not spend that $500 on a new stereo system instead of depositing it into an IRA account? Since we have no specific career goals, why not spend another evening glued to the television screen rather than attending a lecture at a local college? Since we have no specific family goals, why not take the kids to Disneyland again and worry about their college tuition another day? Since we have no specific personal goals, why not deposit our excess funds in a hassle-free, low-interest savings account rather than complicating our existence with CDs and savings bonds?

In the absence of a specific future goal to pursue, the natural human tendency is to respond to a current whim. Unfortunately, we realize only too late that for every whim we have catered to in the past, we have taken one more step away from the achievement of our earlier dreams. What was once a definite possibility is now an irrevocable regret. When you wake up on your fortieth birthday and have only $300 in your savings account, it is too late to recapture your earlier dreams of retiring at 45. When you get a pink slip instead of a paycheck, it is too late to develop a contingency fund. When your eldest son rushes into the room waving an acceptance notice from a leading university, it is too late to make a career change so you will have enough money to help him achieve *his* dreams.

The sad truth is, no matter where you are in life right now, it is already too late to achieve some of your earlier dreams. Even while you are reading these words the clock of life is ticking relentlessly, and with each passing moment another door of future possibilities is silently closing.

Fortunately it is never too late to grab hold of the possibilities that still remain. There is still so much more each of us can do, see, achieve, experience and enjoy if we are but willing to take the time *right now* to design what remains of our lives. We have no time to waste on regret for what might have been as long as there is still time to plan and achieve what still can be.

In his book, *Illusions*[1], Richard Bach writes, "We are never given a wish without also being given the power to make it true." The author then follows this statement with an important caution: "You may have to work for it, however."

---

[1]Richard Bach, *Illusions*, New York: Delacorte Press, 1977.

There is so much we can all achieve if we are prepared to work for it, and part of the work involved in the achievement of our dreams is planning.

HOW TO PLAN THE BALANCE OF YOUR LIFE

Wouldn't it be wonderful if you could sit down right now with paper and pencil and actually design the balance of your life? The truth is, you *can!* With a combination of careful planning and intense, purposeful activity, you *can* create an incredible lifestyle for you and your family in the years ahead. But until you commit your goals to paper and until you develop a specific plan to direct your daily activities, the achievement of those dreams will forever elude you.

In developing a life plan, the first step is to make a list of all of the important things you would like to achieve during your lifetime. While this might seem like a fairly simple task, it may well be one of the most difficult exercises you will be asked to tackle in the financial-planning process.

For most of us, it has been many years since we have given ourselves the liberty and the license to think—really think—about what we want. We have become so involved in the daily routine of how things *are* that we have almost totally lost the ability to dream of how things might one day *be*. Our sense of future vision has been so completely clouded over with current realities that trying to picture how things might be next month is nearly as impossible as trying to envision how we want things to be next year. The urgency of the current moment weighs so heavily on our minds that we have no time or energy to devote to future possibilities. Consequently, we spend our lives like volunteer firefighters running from one crisis to another, never really getting ahead and understanding only when it is far too late where it all went wrong.

There is only one way to prepare for tomorrow's challenges and opportunities, and that is to plan for them today. You cannot prepare for your retirement on your 65th birthday or affect your tax situation on midnight of April 15. Only by seeing future possibilities in advance and preparing for them over the course of several months or several years can you make your life work out the way you want it to.

In Exercise 7–1, make a list of all of the future dreams you would like to achieve and all of the future possibilities for which you would like to be prepared. Do not worry about establishing priorities, weighing the risks or even considering the odds of achieving these goals. The important thing for the moment is to capture a vision of the future—*your* future—on paper. Under each of the major headings we have listed topics in the left-hand column to help direct your thinking. After you have reviewed these items, write down your actual goals in the right-hand column.

Exercise 7–1
Personal Financial Goals

A. PERSONAL GOALS	
Assets/possessions	
Career changes/achievements	
Travel	
Education	
Lifestyle	
Definition of financial independence	
B. FINANCIAL GOALS	
Major purchases	
Reduction of debt	
Reduction of taxes	
Investments/increase assets	

Exercise 7–1 continued

Savings program
Standard of living
Reallocation of income
Net worth
Contingency funds

C. PROVIDING FOR MY FAMILY
Insurance
Education
Standard of living
Travel/vacation home
Assets for estate
Medical/dental

D. RETIREMENT PLANS
Age
Standard of living
Location/type of residence
Lifestyle
Full or partial retirement
Sources of retirement income

E. ESTATE PLANS
Your will
Trust funds
Beneficiaries
Distribution of assets
Nature of assets
Charitable contributions

UNDERSTANDING YOUR OPTIONS

As a human being you were born with a miraculous gift called "choice," a gift that is waiting at this very moment to be exercised and implemented. In fact, the whole fabric of your current existence is woven from the threads of past choices—choices you have made either overtly with conscious thought and decision or choices you have made covertly through your silence, your acceptance, your resignation. Whether you have saved or not saved; whether you have tried or not tried; whether you have planned or not planned; whether you have invested or not invested—all of these events came about as a result of human choice.

In the final analysis, anyone who has ever said, "I have no choice" is denying themselves a fundamental human right. We *always* have a choice. If you want you *can* quit your job tomorrow. If the idea appeals to you, you can also choose *not* to pay your taxes or your creditors. You can eat chocolate until you are sick, cheat on your spouse, lie to your kids, and even rob a bank, if you are so inclined. The only thing that holds you back from making certain choices is the perceived negative consequences associated with them.

In other words, while the idea of taking care of our financial needs once and for all by robbing a bank has a certain appeal, the potential legal and moral consequences of that action cause us to choose other methods of meeting our financial requirements.

Often, we fail to make effective financial and personal choices in our lives simply because we do not use our ability to perceive future consequences beyond immediate circumstances. For example, when a couple in their early thirties is choosing between buying a second car or saving for their children's education, they are far more likely to opt for the car. The negative consequences of *not* having one seem far more real than the negative consequences of not having enough money for future tuition at Harvard or Princeton. Only when that bitter day of reckoning finally arrives will they realize their mistake. Unfortunately, it will be too late then to fix the past.

Our natural tendency is to base the majority of our decisions and choices on the consequences of the immediate future rather than the consequences of more distant years. The reason is simple: It is much easier to experience the reality of the consequence when it is closer to home. In the example given earlier, the hassle and inconvenience of having only one car to drive seems much more real (and therefore much more pressing) than the pain and disappointment the couple may one day experience when they have to tell their children that they can't afford to send them to college.

In order to become better financial managers and life planners, we must learn to think much further into the future. At the very least, we must try at all times to consider the consequences of our choices and our actions over the course of the next 5 to 10 years. By projecting at least five years into the future and weighing potential consequences as they will be then, more effective decisions become much easier today. For example, if you are currently in your early thirties, an opportunity for a management position with your company may have very little meaning. After all, that type of career advancement doesn't usually occur until after your fortieth birthday. As a result, you may choose to spend your evenings playing cards with friends in order to satisfy current social needs rather than taking night courses to guarantee the achievement of future career goals. Much sooner than you think, however, your fortieth birthday will arrive and then your forty-first . . . and your forty-second . . . and your dream about a vice-presidency will have been achieved by someone else who had the foresight to plan for the future. While you were passing your time satisfying current needs, the new vice president was investing time in the achievement of future goals.

Regardless what choices we make, there is inevitably something to be gained and something to be given up. The key is to look far enough down the road to be able to weigh *that* picture against the consequences of any current gains or losses. In the light of that future view, the pain of being passed over for the promotion would probably seem more alarming than the prospect of missing out on a few evenings with friends.

If we were to ask you right now to make a list of the things you consider to be priorities based on your current feelings, you would probably choose items associated with the immediate future such as a new car, summer vacation with the family, and so forth. What we would like you to do now is to stretch your thinking beyond the next 12 months and imagine yourself (and your family) at least five or 10 years into the future. See the consequences of your failure to plan well in advance. Feel the emotions of those moments, the good and the bad. Then, using this future vision to direct your thoughts, refer to the list of goals you wrote down in Exercise 7–1 and select the specific items you consider to be the most important objectives for you to begin to work toward achieving. Write them in the blanks in Exercise 7–2.

Exercise 7–2
Personal Priorities

______________________________	$ __________
______________________________	$ __________
______________________________	$ __________
______________________________	$ __________
______________________________	$ __________
______________________________	$ __________
______________________________	$ __________
______________________________	$ __________
______________________________	$ __________
______________________________	$ __________

Next, assign an estimated dollar amount to each goal based on the actual cash required to achieve it. For example, if one of your priorities is to purchase a new house, you don't need to write down the total price of the home since it will be assumed that part of the purchase price will be financed by a mortgage loan. Instead, write down the actual amount of cash you will need to cover the down payment, settlement costs, moving expenses, and so forth. If your goal is to purchase a $100,000 life insurance policy, then write down the estimated cost of the annual premiums, and so forth.

Finally, following the time chart in Table 7–1, establish a deadline date for achieving each of these goals. Then complete the chart in Exercise 7–3 for your own financial goals, using all the information you have compiled to this point. Take into account the number of years you have to achieve your goal and average rates of return you can expect if you were to invest those dollars as shown in our illustration for the Smith family. Refer to Table

Table 7–1
Smith Family's Personal and Financial Goals

Goal	Total Funds Required	Number of Years	Annual Funds Required*
4-Bedroom home	$25,000	5	$3,725
Education funds	30,000	15	860
Contingency fund	6,000	5	895
Life insurance	1,500	1	1,500
Elimination of debt	4,500	5	670
Update current will	500	1	500
Second car	15,000	6	2,200
Condo in Florida for vacations and retirement	20,000	20	320
Own business	50,000	15	1,430
Total Annual Requirements			12,100

*Assuming a 10% return on annual investment.

Exercise 7–3
Your Personal and Financial Goals

Goal	Total Funds Required	Number of Years	Annual Funds Required*
	$		$
Total Annual Requirements			$

*Assuming a ____ % return on annual investment.

6–1 to determine the approximate annual funds required to achieve each goal. For the moment, do not worry about whether or not you will have adequate funds to achieve the goal within the allotted time frame. Simply get the facts down on paper first.

NEXT STEPS

Now that your personal goals and priorities for the next five to ten years (and possibly even beyond) have been identified, your personal financial planner can work with you to chart out a course for achieving those goals. In the next chapter we will reexamine current income and expenditures and determine the specific amount of additional income that will be required from other sources to make your current dreams become future realities.

Part 3
Developing Your Financial Plan

8
Analysis of Your Current Direction

THE DOLLARS

Ultimately, there are only three ways in which to provide the required surplus funds to achieve your goals:

Increase your monthly income

Decrease your monthly expenditures

Reevaluate your goals and priorities

Increasing Your Monthly Income

Unfortunately, very few of us are in a position to walk into our employer's office tomorrow morning and demand a raise to meet our short- and long-term needs. And even if we were to receive a raise in pay, the chances are that the increase would merely keep us at par with the current rate of inflation or place us in a higher tax bracket. Figures 8–1 and 8–2 graphically depict the "real" results of increases in income.

Figure 8–1
Consumer Price Index Since 1979*

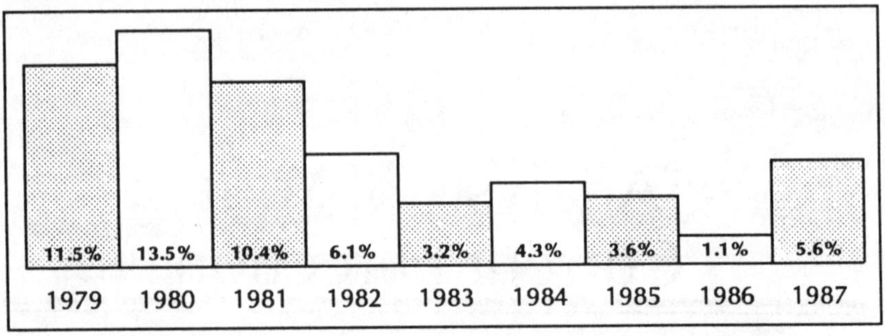

**Statistical Abstracts of the United States*, United States Bureau of Census: 1987.

For example, John Brown's salary in 1986 was $27,000. In 1987 he received a 10 percent salary increase. Mr. Brown is single and has no itemized deductions.

As you can see, with an increase in taxes and the inflation rate factored in, Mr. Brown's actual pay increase amounts to approximately $37.31 or 2 percent—not enough for a night on the town

Figure 8–2
Net Gain From 10 Percent Pay Raise

Before Raise		
Monthly Gross Income	$2,250.00	
Federal Taxes	– 382.73	
Monthly Net Income	$1,867.27	
After Raise		
Monthly Gross Income	$2,475.00	
Federal Taxes	– 446.67	
Inflation Factor (5%)	– 123.75	
Monthly Net Income	$1,904.58	
Actual Monthly Increase	$37.31	(2%)

let alone the dollars needed to create future financial independence.

Just as we tend to be misled by the value of the proverbial annual raise, so too do many married couples misjudge the value of a second income.

Figure 8–3 illustrates such a situation. In order to augment the family's income, Mrs. Johnson decides to go back to work in 1987. Her husband, Bill, is currently earning $40,000 a year. Mrs. Johnson's job will provide a gross annual income of $25,000 a year. The Johnson's have two preschool children and no itemized deductions.

What appeared to be a monthly increase of $2000 actually nets out to just a little over $200! And by the time you factor in state tax,

Figure 8–3
Net Gain From Second Income

Before Second Income	
Bill's Monthly Gross Income	$3,333.33
Federal Taxes	– 545.25
Bill's Monthly Net Income	$2,788.08
After Second Income	
Combined Monthly Gross Income	$5,416.67
Federal Taxes	– 1,339.87
Combined Monthly Net Income	$4,076.80
Additional Monthly Employment Expenses:	
Transportation	– 120.00
Clothing/Personal Care/Cleaning	– 150.00
Babysitter/Day Care	– 600.00
Housekeeper	– 100.00
Meals (lunches at work, etc.)	– 100.00
Effective Monthly Net Income	$3,006.80
Total Monthly Increase with Second Income of $25,000 per Annum	$218.72

FICA and so forth, the true impact of Mrs. Johnson's income on the family budget is probably nil. Does this mean that a nonworking spouse should stay at home instead of seeking employment? Not at all. Sometimes the psychic income to be derived from gainful employment (e.g., self-confidence, creativity, personal challenge, etc.) is worth more than the dollars and cents of a paycheck. However, if the only reason a spouse is considering going back to work is financial, then the impact of that potential additional income should be weighed carefully against additional monthly overhead, loss of tax deductions and/or a subsequent increase in taxes to determine whether or not the second income will achieve the desired results.

Since a raise in pay or a second income is not always the best solution to the need for a monthly increase in working capital, what can you do to create surplus funds?

Fortunately, a good financial planner can usually find dozens of ways to increase your operating capital through tax planning and a carefully constructed investment portfolio. But for the moment, let's concentrate on the things that you can do to supplement the efforts of your financial planner.

Go for Perks Rather than Pennies

By the time inflation and the IRS are finished with your annual raise there's seldom enough of an increase in your weekly paycheck to make a noticeable difference. For this reason, consider opting for company perks rather than pay hikes whenever possible. Following is a list of some of the alternatives that might be negotiated with your employer. Be sure to review the tax consequences with your financial planner or accountant before making the final choice.

1. **Employee Expenses.** If you have been paying your own job-related expenses, you might consider passing up your raise in exchange for a company-paid expense account. Since the 1986 tax laws impose numerous restrictions on the business expenses you can deduct (e.g., only those expenses that

exceed 2 percent of your adjusted gross income are deductible), you will probably come out ahead by having your employer pick up the tab.

2. **Life Insurance or Medical/Dental Insurance.** Tax reform allows company-paid health plans and up to $50,000 worth of group term life insurance coverage to remain tax-free.
3. **Stock Options.** Stock options are not as valuable as they once were due to the loss of the preferential long-term capital gains treatment. However, since no gains are incurred until the option is actually exercised, they are still an effective method of deferring taxable income.
4. **Pension Plan Contributions.** If you are single and your adjusted gross income is less than $25,000, or if you are married and your combined adjusted gross income is less than $40,000, you can still have your cake and eat it too. In other words, you would still be eligible to take advantage of the maximum IRA deduction even if you are also participating in an employer-sponsored pension plan.
5. **Gifts and Awards.** Under the new tax laws, all gifts of up to $400 and certain gifts of up to $1600 given to employees in recognition of outstanding achievements, length of service, and so forth will be excluded from taxation. Why not let your employer pick up the tab for the new refrigerator you need via a bonus instead of his showing appreciation for your services by raising your paycheck?

Investigate Tax-Advantaged Income

Another way to augment your income is to develop a business of your own. Your business could start on a part-time basis and eventually develop into a full-time career.

For many people self-employment has great appeal. Couples approaching retirement appreciate the additional income their part-time efforts provide and the sense of joint purpose their business gives them once they have retired. Younger couples enjoy being able to set their own hours so they have more time to devote to their growing children. Others find that a business on the side provides a sense of security in an era of employee cutbacks and layoffs.

The income derived from self-employment offers some very attractive tax benefits as well. Many of your current monthly expenses often become legitimate business deductions. For example, if you run your business from your home, a percentage of your rent, computer, utilities, insurance, telephone, and so forth may be deductible. Between business write-offs and depreciation schedules, the self-employed can make themselves look as poor as church mice on their tax returns while making regular deposits into their bank accounts.

The start-up costs for a small business range from under a hundred dollars to over $100,000 depending on the nature of the enterprise. As with most small businesses, you should anticipate running at a loss, or at best break-even, for the first 12 to 24 months. Thereafter, you may realize some very substantial financial and personal returns.

Invest in Yourself

A quality education in today's marketplace is no longer considered to be an attribute—it is virtually a requirement.

Education can be a very expensive and time-consuming process, but it can and will pay for itself many times over in the years ahead. In addition to providing you with more attractive employment opportunities, a degree in a progressive field from a recognized college can also provide you with added job security.

Whether you elect to return to school as a full-time or part-time student, and whether you choose to learn a new skill or pursue a degree program, be sure to examine your options carefully. Make sure you investigate the costs in terms of both time and money, the ranking or reputation of the institution, and the long-term job market for a particular area of study before you make any final decisions.

Use Credit/Leverage Effectively

As discussed in Chapter 6, credit can be an incredible asset when properly managed. It allows you to use someone else's money to generate additional cash flow, create additional profits, or save substantially on high-ticket items by purchasing at a discount.

Used wisely, your good credit rating can enable you to achieve your financial goals without forcing you to drastically alter your current lifestyle. For example, suppose you are in your late 20s, married, and have two children ages 1 and 3. On your list of goals you have assigned the following three items an equal priority:

Purchase a 3-bedroom home in 2.5 years

Begin saving for children's college education

Begin saving for early retirement at age 55

After working out the dollars and cents required for these three equally important goals, you have determined you will need approximately $10,000 in cash to cover the down payment and closing costs on a new home, approximately $50,000 in 15 years time to send your children to quality institutions, and approximately $300,000 in additional cash and investments to meet your living expenses comfortably in 25 years based on current rates of inflation. To achieve these goals Figure 8–4 shows you how much money you must save on a monthly basis.

Figure 8–4
Monthly Savings Needed to Meet Goals

Goal	Required Monthly Savings*
New Home	$310
College Education	120
Retirement Fund	230
Total Required Monthly Savings	$660

*Assuming a 10% annual return on your investment.

Unfortunately, with your current income and overhead, you have only $500 in surplus funds to invest in your better future. Does this mean that one of your goals will have to be abandoned? Not at all. Assuming you maintain your good credit status, there are a number of ways in which you can achieve all three goals with a combination of financial juggling and leverage.

For example, you could eliminate the savings program you intended for your children's college tuition and plan instead to borrow against the equity in your home to fund their education. With even minimal annual appreciation on your residence, there is almost certain to be sufficient equity in the property to cover all, or at the very least, a major portion of the education expenses.

By the same token, even if you set aside only 80 percent of your monthly requirements for your early retirement (i.e., $184 a month) in 15 years there would be over $70,000 in that savings plan—more than enough to provide sufficient collateral for a college education loan. Granted, in order to meet your retirement goal you would have to save nearly 520 percent of the amount you have currently scheduled each month during the 10 years immediately preceding your planned retirement (i.e., $1425 a month for 10 years versus $230 a month for 25 years.) However, by then you would be entering your peak earning years, and with your children away from the nest, your monthly expenses could be considerably lower as well.

Obviously, there are a number of disadvantages in financing your dreams with borrowed funds, not least of which is the additional cost. For example, if you borrow $50,000 against your home for 15 years at 14 percent to fund your children's education, the finance charges will amount to nearly $70,000, with monthly payments in excess of $660! However, by assuming the additional expense at a time in life when your increased salary will likely allow you to meet this increased overhead comfortably, it may be worthwhile to pay the higher price in order to have the satisfaction of achieving the goal.

The important thing to realize is that using your good credit does offer you some additional options if you are willing to pay the price. Leverage also can be used effectively in conjunction

Table 8–1
Comparison of Saving vs. Borrowing for Children's Education

Amount Saved in Advance	Monthly Deposit Required	Total Funds Deposited	Approx. Value of Funds after 15 yrs.*
100%	$120	$21,600	$50,000
75%	90	16,200	37,500
50%	60	10,800	25,000
25%	30	5,400	12,500
0%	0	0	0

*Assuming 10% annual return on deposits

Amount Borrowed	Monthly Loan Payment*	Total Loan Payments	Actual Out-of-Pocket Expenses**
$ 0	$ 0	$ 0	$ 21,600
12,500	166	29,880	46,080
25,000	333	59,940	70,740
37,500	499	89,820	95,220
50,000	666	119,880	119,800

* 15-year term loan at 14 percent

** Total Funds Deposited + Total Loan Payments = Actual Out-of-Pocket Expense incurred to fund education.

with a savings program. For example, you might opt to save 50 percent of the cost of your children's education in advance and finance the remainder when the tuition bills actually start to roll in. Table 8–1 shows you the inherent costs of financing your dreams rather than saving for them.

Decreasing Your Monthly Expenditures

Since there is a limit to the number of years you have left to achieve your financial goals, and since there is a limit on the maximum return you can anticipate from any investment, it is important to pinpoint some specific target areas that could or perhaps should be reduced in order to create additional surplus funds each month to invest in your financial future.

1. **Cut Back Instead of Cutting Out.** Making cutbacks in your monthly expenditures will undoubtedly have some impact on your current lifestyle. In order to achieve most of your goals, some sacrifices probably will be necessary. Even if your solution is to increase your income rather than decrease your expenses, there still will be a price to be paid. An increase in salary usually goes hand in hand with additional responsibilities and a longer work week, which in turn has its own, often undesirable, impact on your current lifestyle.

   Fortunately, it is much easier to cut back than it is to cut out. By doing a little budget trimming you can still enjoy your current lifestyle while at the same time generating sufficient surplus funds to achieve your dreams.

   If you have difficulty trying to decide how to go about trimming your monthly budget, then try placing yourself in the following hypothetical situation. Suppose your present employer has had a particularly bad year because of a downturn in the economy. Instead of giving you an annual raise, you and all of the other employees are asked to take a 10 percent pay cut for the next three years. Assuming you agree to this proposition rather than seeking employment elsewhere, what adjustments would you make to your spending habits so that you could survive on this reduced salary? Write the budget items and proposed savings in Exercise 8–1.

2. **Accelerate the Achievement of Short-Term Goals.** Another effective way of achieving your goals when you have a limited amount of surplus capital to invest is to juggle the time frame and the dollar allotments you have assigned to each goal. Let's go back to our earlier example and see how taking this approach can work effectively for you.

   As you will recall, the three goals you want to achieve are buying a new home (2.5 years), saving $50,000 for your children's education (15 years) and saving $300,000 for your early retirement (25 years). The dollar allotment and time frame for achieving those goals is shown in Table 8–2.

   The major problem with this plan is that you need at least

Exercise 8–1
10% Cutback in Living Expenses

Adjustments	$ Savings

Total Additional Funds Created by Cutbacks $ ______

Table 8–2
Dollars and Time for Achieving Financial Goals*

Years	New Home	College Fund	Retirement Fund	Monthly
25	$0	$0	$230	$230
15	0	120	230	350
10	0	120	230	350
5	0	120	230	350
4	0	120	230	350
3	0	120	230	350
2.5	310	120	230	660
2	310	120	230	660
1	310	120	230	660
0	310	120	230	660

* Assuming a 10% annual return on your investment

Table 8–3
Reallocated Dollars and Time for Achieving Financial Goals*

Years	New Home	College Fund	Retirement Fund	Monthly
25	$0	$0	$315	$315
15	0	155	315	470
10	0	155	315	470
5	0	155	315	470
4	0	155	315	470
3	0	155	315	470
2	0	155	315	470
1.5	500	0	0	500
1	500	0	0	500
0	500	0	0	500

*Assuming a 10% annual return on your investment.

$660 a month to make the plan work and your surplus funds amount to only $500 a month. By rearranging the dollar amounts and the time frame for each of these goals you can still achieve all three objectives without going over your $500 budget or borrowing money from the bank (Table 8–3).

The key to making this plan work is staying on target. The moment we give ourselves the liberty to postpone saving for a specific future goal for a year or two, we run the inherent risk of never following through on our commitment. Inevitably something else pops up in the next 12 to 24 months that causes us to postpone implementing our earlier plan by another year . . . or two . . . or three.

One of the advantages of working with a good financial planner is that he or she will monitor your financial progress at least once a year. If you fail to follow the recommendations of the plan thoroughly, or if the yields on your investments are significantly higher or lower than previously anticipated, the planner will be able to evaluate the impact of your procrastination or the effect of these rate fluctuations and recommend specific corrective measures.

THE SENSE

There are two sides to every story, and the story of personal financial planning is no exception. So far we have examined the factual side, namely the dollars required to achieve your goals. Now it is time to take a look at the other side of the coin—the side that deals with the human emotions and the real-life practicalities of making our dreams come true.

Wants vs. Needs

Although taxation and inflation take their toll on our financial well-being, there is one other factor that affects us far more seriously than these two combined—personal consumption.

It has wisely been said that what you earn is far less important than what you *do* with what you earn. While it is true that our net income certainly affects our lifestyle, it is also true that the way in which we manage those funds affects our lifestyle a great deal more.

Have you ever noticed that no matter how sizable your paycheck becomes it disappears just as quickly as it did before your last raise? Granted, some of the "disappearing act" may be a result of increased taxes or inflation, but primarily it is a result of unchecked personal spending. You see, our income may change, but unless our spending habits change as well, we simply buy more or spend more than we did before. We buy more clothes or better clothes. We buy another car or a new car. We buy more restaurant meals or better restaurant meals. And we keep on spending more or buying better until once again our income is just barely enough to meet our monthly expenses.

In order to get a better handle on your spending habits, it is important to understand the driving force behind your decision to buy. As consumers we purchase things primarily on the basis of a perceived *need*. For example, we may buy a home because we *need* a place to live or we may buy a car because we *need* transportation. But the reason why we buy a particular home or a certain automobile has nothing whatsoever to do with needs. The choices we make to fulfill these needs are generally influenced by personal values. The purchase of a new home may fulfill a human requirement for shelter, but the fact that the house we buy has an inground swimming pool, a two-car garage, and a panoramic view has very little to do with what we *need* and everything to do with what we *want*.

Personal consumption can best be controlled by a careful examination of the various factors that may be influencing our buying decisions. High on this list of consumption persuaders are advertisements and peer pressure. Rare is the individual who can resist the temptation to "keep up with the Joneses"—regardless of the cost. Yet, in our desire to keep pace with our peers and the changing times, far too often our personal goals become the sacrificial lambs laid upon the altar of style, fashion, and passing fads.

The best way to overcome this tendency to spend unnecessarily or excessively is to constantly weigh the value of the purchase against the value of your goals. And if the positive pull of the future doesn't seem to do the trick, then mentally contrast how you will feel if you don't purchase a particular item today versus how you will feel if you become unemployed, chained to an unfulfilling job for the next 30 years, broke, unable to provide your family with the things they deserve, or are still living in that same two-bedroom "starter home" hopelessly in debt.

Strengthening Your Weaknesses

If you have difficulty sticking to a budget or lack the discipline to save a fixed amount on a regular basis then take heart—you are certainly not alone. There are millions of Americans who have exactly the same problem, which is why so many of us end up in such deplorable financial circumstances.

The truth is that if you haven't learned to budget and save by now, you probably never will. Let's face it—you're just that kind of person, and the sooner you recognize how you really are, the sooner you can do something about it.

1. **Appoint Your Own Controller.** In the business world, every successful company has a financial overseer who goes by the title of accountant or controller. The primary function of this individual is to develop a budget and cash flow projections for the company so that spending doesn't get out of hand. The fact that there is enough money in the company till every month to meet payroll, pay the rent and utilities, and meet the hundreds of other expenses the company incurs as part of its overhead structure is usually attributable to the fact that someone has managed those funds in a way that is consistent with the both the short-term needs and long-term objectives of the company. If budgeting isn't your style, then find someone who can do the job for you. Whether you enlist your spouse, your parents, your accountant, your best friend, or your brother-in-law to act as your personal controller is completely up to you. The key thing is to find someone who will keep you on the right financial track.
2. **You Can't Spend What You Don't Have.** If you have the best intentions to save a certain amount every month but the worst track record when it comes to actually doing it why not have the amount deducted from your paycheck or your bank account automatically? Many companies offer savings and pension plans to their employees as part of the standard benefits package. Usually, a quick visit to the personnel department and your signature on the dotted line is all it requires to arrange for a specific sum to be deducted from

your paycheck each month and deposited into a savings account or pension fund. Many banks offer a similar type of service. You can arrange for the bank to deduct a specific amount from your personal account every month for redeposit into a special savings or IRA account.

3. **Family Council.** One of the reasons it is often difficult to follow through with our plans is because no one else seems to understand or appreciate what is is that we are trying to do. If you are single, then the success or failure of your plan falls entirely on your capable shoulders. However, if you are married and have a family, then be prepared for the fact that family members can wreak havoc on your plan in a single 24-hour period.

   To avoid this eventuality, schedule a "family council" before putting your plan into effect. By explaining the purpose of the plan, the benefits, and the specific support you require from each family member to make the plan work, you will be more likely to receive the cooperation you need to achieve your goals.

Values vs. Valuables

One final but important piece of advice concerning your goal list: Make sure it reflects intangible values as well as tangible valuables. In other words, make sure you have given ample consideration to your personal dreams as well as your financial desires. As Thoreau wisely observed, "Money is not required to buy one necessity of the soul." Far too often financial goals are achieved at the expense of personal values. Therefore, great caution should be exercised at all times lest in the pursuit of what you *do* want to have you become someone you *don't* want to be. A good plan and a good planner should help you not only earn more and save more, but also realize more and become more as a human being.

Exercise 8–2
Working with Your Planner—Summary Checklist

Before

( ) Examine your personal spending habits very closely.

( ) Consider ways of increasing your income or decreasing your expenses. The more you give your planner to work with, the more he or she can do for you.

( ) Be sure to list your personal goals in order of priority.

( ) Discuss the importance of personal financial planning with your family. Help them to understand how the plan will work to everyone's benefit. Also be sure to discuss ways in which you will need their support and cooperation to achieve certain goals.

During

( ) Be prepared to put a tighter rein on your spending habits. In order to make the plan work, you are going to have to follow it closely and consistently.

( ) If you have difficulty making regular contributions to a savings or investment program, ask your planner to assist you in finding the most practical way to guarantee that the necessary deposits will be made.

( ) Be flexible regarding low priority goals and firm regarding high priority goals. Remember, this is your financial plan and your life. Your planner doesn't have to agree with your goals; he or she merely has to find a way to achieve them wherever possible.

(continued)

Exercise 8–2 continued

After

( ) Once you have agreed to them, implement the recommendations of the plan immediately.

( ) Consult with your planner at least once a year to review your financial progress.

( ) If circumstances change or require you to deviate from the plan, be sure to discuss the impact of these changes will your planner.

9
Risk Management

THE DOLLARS

Although the primary objective of personal financial planning is to increase your net worth, it is equally important to *protect* your net worth as well. For this reason, risk management plays a key role in the planning process.

In financial planning terms, "risk" can be defined as any circumstance or condition that has the capacity to erode or destroy your financial well-being. Following this definition, there are two areas of potential risk against which we must guard ourselves: loss of income and loss of assets.

Loss of Income

Basically, there are three ways in which you might lose your current source of income: being laid off, being laid up, or being laid out. You must guard your assets, therefore, against the possibilities of unemployment, prolonged illness or permanent disability, and premature death.

Unemployment

Someone once defined a job as "something at which you work just hard enough to keep from being fired and for which your employer pays you just enough to prevent you from quitting." But no matter how you define the word, for most of us a job is the principal source of our personal income. And since most of our current needs and long-range goals are inherent in these weekly paychecks, the income we earn from employment is certainly worth protecting.

There are three ways we can minimize the potential risk and negative financial impact of unemployment. First, we can become more valuable to our current employer. Whether this means putting in longer hours, shouldering additional responsibilities, increasing our results, or learning new skills will depend on your current employment situation. The key thing to remember is that we are paid not for the *hours* we spend on the job, but rather for the *value* derived from those hours. In other words, anyone can put in 40 hours a week behind a desk. What ultimately determines your value to the company is what you accomplish during that time.

Second, we must be prepared for the fact that regardless of our value, unemployment can strike at any time. Companies go under or change ownership every day. And even if your company remains intact, you may find yourself replaced by someone 20 years your junior who is willing to do the same job for half the pay. A sluggish economy could cause departmental cutbacks or major layoffs.

Ultimately, no matter how well you perform or how valuable you may be, there are no guarantees in the employment game. For this reason, you should be prepared—financially, psychologically and professionally—for the unexpected at all times. Even if you have no plans or desires to leave your current employer, it doesn't hurt to keep your eyes and ears open regarding job openings in your local community and in other cities. If you get a pink slip instead of a paycheck next week, your creditors aren't going to give you additional time to wallow in self-pity. You need to act and act fast to find a new source of income. And to keep you comfortably afloat if the ship ever sinks beneath you, a contingency account should be one of your top financial priorities.

Most experts recommend having the equivalent of at least six months' income in some kind of highly liquid (i.e., easily accessible) investment or savings account to tide you over until a new job is found. Of course the size of your contingency fund will be determined in large part by the nature of the job you are seeking. If you have the good fortune of being in a field where there are more jobs available than people to fill them, you may require a safety margin of only one or two months' income. By the same token, if you are in a limited employment field or if you are a highly paid executive in your late 50s, you might be well advised to increase your fund to provide a comfortable income for 10 to 12 months. In any event, your planner should work with you to determine both the required amount and the best form of liquid assets to cushion against such an eventuality.

Finally, you can follow the recommendations outlined in previous chapters and invest in your own education or develop a second career or sideline business that could become a full-time occupation if necessary.

Prolonged Illness or Disability

While most people carry some form of life insurance, less than 20 percent of all Americans are adequately covered against the possibility of long-term illness or permanent disability. And yet, according to the statistics, the chances of becoming temporarily or permanently disabled in your lifetime are nearly twice as great as the risk of premature death. It is estimated that, between the ages of 35 and 65, one out of every three individuals will suffer some form of disability lasting at least 90 days. With these odds, truly none of us can afford to ignore this risk or its potentially devastating impact on our financial well-being.

One of the primary reasons most people elect to run the risks rather than insure against them is that medical and disability insurance policies are very expensive. In fact, in the last decade, health insurance costs have risen as much as 35 percent a year! For example, in 1977 annual health care costs for the elderly were only $698. By 1986, these costs had risen to $1791 a year—a total increase of approximately 157 percent in less than 10 years.[1] But when you consider the staggering cost of even a simple operation, the annual premiums seem incidental by comparison.

Fortunately, most employees receive fairly comprehensive medical coverage through employer-paid or supplemented group plans. These plans offer relatively extensive coverage to employees and their families at rates considerably lower then they would have to pay to receive the same insurance benefits through private coverage. However, every plan has its limits, and it is a good idea to investigate the limits of your current insurance plan and consider supplementing it if need be. Although a good financial planner will review your medical benefits in detail and make recommendations regarding supplemental coverage, following are a few items you may want to examine yourself in the interim.

Does the plan cover *all* family members? Many plans do not cover college-age children.

How high are the annual deductibles? Annual deductibles are the expenses that must be paid by the insured before the policy coverage goes into effect. Annual deductibles may be as low as $100 or as high as $1000 a year.

Is there a co-insurance clause in the the policy? For example, the insurance company may pay only 80 percent of the costs up to the first $5000 and then 100 percent of the cost thereafter. The insured would have to pay the 20 percent on the first $5000.

---

[1]*Source:* Health Care Financing Administration

Does the policy offer any conversion privileges? Some policies allow you to convert automatically to an individual policy without medical examination should you leave your current employer. If you plan to take an early retirement and/or you or your spouse should become a poor medical risk, this conversion privilege could be an important factor.

Are the plan aggregates generally high enough? The aggregates are the total amounts that an insurance company will pay, per individual, throughout the life of the policy. Often these lifetime aggregates are broken into specific categories. For example, the lifetime maximum on accidents and/or illnesses may be $1,000,000 while the lifetime maximums on mental illnesses or nervous disorders may only be $5000 or $10,000.

What hospital and surgical benefits does the plan cover? Be sure to read the fine print regarding surgery and associated costs, hospital care, intensive care, out-patient care, private nursing or at-home care, pregnancy and maternity benefits, and so forth. Also be sure to examine the annual or lifetime maximums for each type of medical care.

Are there any particular illnesses or medical costs that are not covered? Aside from self-inflicted injuries, are there any other medical problems that are excluded from coverage such as health-care costs associated with cancer or mental illness?

In all probability, the major medical policy offered through your current employer will require only minimal supplemental coverage to give you full protection. Instead, the primary focus of your attention and your insurance dollars are probably best directed at long-term disability or income continuation policies.

The purpose of this type of insurance is to provide you with a continuing source of income in the event of short-term or permanent disability resulting from accident or illness. Although many employees have disability coverage through workers' compensation, this coverage extends only to work-related injuries and the actual dollar compensation may not replace the wage earner's salary. For this reason, some additional form of disability insurance should be purchased.

When purchasing disability insurance, there are five primary factors to be considered. First, the definition of the term "disability" itself. In most instances you will want to select a policy that defines disability as an inability to perform your *own* occupation as opposed to *any* occupation. According to the latter definition, if you are capable of performing *any* occupation whatsoever, the full coverage would not apply.

Many policies also contain what is known as a "split definition." For example, they might define disability as being unable to perform your own occupation for the first 24 months and any occupation thereafter. Be especially wary of any hidden "prison clauses" in the policy. A prison clause is so-called because, according to the definition of the term, the disabled individual must be confined indoors or to the house at all times.

Second, be certain that you select a policy that covers you for disability resulting from either accident *or* illness. Many policies provide coverage for only one or the other.

Third, whenever possible, select the longest elimination or waiting period to reduce your premiums. The elimination or waiting period refers to the specific time after the disabling accident or illness occurs before the insurance company actually begins to pay the benefits. Waiting periods are usually 30, 90, or 180 days. By selecting the maximum waiting period you can often reduce your monthly premiums substantially.

Fourth, be sure you understand the exact amount of coverage the policy will provide. Participation-limit policies are generally less expensive because they guarantee a specific monthly payment based on all combined benefits you are receiving. For example, if the policy guaranteed you an income of $2000 a month and you were receiving $250 from a state disability program and $600 a month from workers' compensation, the actual amount you would receive from the insurance company would be $1150 ($250 + $600 + $1150 = $2000). Issue-limit policies, on the other hand, pay a fixed monthly benefit regardless of any other compensation you may be receiving.

Finally, be sure you are covered for both short-term and long-term disability as well as partial or full disability.

To help minimize some of the costs of short-term disability insurance you might want to consider some of the products currently being offered by various credit card and health insurance companies. For only a few dollars a month you can obtain a policy that would make your minimum monthly payments to your creditors for up to 9 months if you are unemployed or until the balance is paid in full if you become permanently disabled. By the same token, for a relatively low, fixed monthly payment, you can receive up to $250 a day for each day you are in the hospital to help offset a temporary loss of income or medical costs not covered by your current health plan.

Whatever policies or supplemental plans you choose, be sure to shop around for those offering maximum benefits for minimum insurance dollars. With so many competitive products on the market these days, it pays to examine as many as you can before making your final selection.

Premature Death of Wage-Earner

The amount of life insurance you should purchase and the type of policy you should select will depend entirely on who you want to provide for and how you want to provide for them. In the final analysis, your answer to both of these questions will undoubtedly change a few dozen times throughout the course of your life. For this reason, life insurance, like all other forms of risk coverage, should never be considered a one-time purchase. Instead, both the amount and type of coverage should be reviewed every two or three years.

When choosing a life insurance policy, begin by identifying the objectives you would like to achieve. Use Exercise 9-1 to check off the specific personal objectives that are most relevant to your current family circumstances and financial needs and that could be met best through life insurance.

Exercise 9–1
Life Insurance Objectives

( ) Provide lifetime living expenses for surviving spouse of principal wage-earner

( ) Provide support for surviving dependents of principal wage-earner through age _____

( ) Provide support for surviving dependent parents/relatives

( ) Provide sufficient funds to offset loss of income due to premature death of secondary wage-earner

( ) Provide sufficient funds to offset increased household maintenance and/or child-care expenses that would be incurred in the event of premature death of nonworking spouse

( ) Provide lump-sum cash inheritance for beneficiaries

( ) Pay off existing mortgage on family residence

( ) Pay off all outstanding debts, loans, bills, etc.

( ) Provide adequate living expenses for survivors of principal wage earner during period of estate settlement

( ) Provide sufficient cash to cover funeral/burial expenses

( ) Provide sufficient funds for education of all dependent children

( ) Provide sufficient funds to meet requirements of buy-sell agreements for closely held business interests/partnerships

Exercise 9–1 continued

( ) Other ____

____

( ) Other ____

____

Based on the objectives you have selected, your financial planner will be able to determine the specific amount of life insurance you will require to meet your needs.

In some instances, the funds required will be met by a lump-sum cash payment. For example, if one of your objectives is to pay off an outstanding mortgage, the insurance required would be the exact amount of the existing mortgage.

In other cases, the amount of insurance required will be based on a number of important variables. For example, if your goal is to provide lifetime support for your spouse, your planner will have to take into account the percentage of your current income that will be required to support your surviving spouse during the time when dependent children are still at home and during the period when your children have left the nest. Generally, if you have no major debts or mortgage to consider, 60-to-65 percent of your current income will be adequate. However, if your surviving spouse will also be required to meet mortgage payments or other major debts, lifetime payments equal to 75 or 80 percent of your current income might be more appropriate. Next, the planner must factor in prevailing and projected rates of interest. The amount of interest earned by the policy or the cash proceeds will affect the face value amount required. And third, your planner will have to take into consideration both the life expectancy of the surviving spouse as well as the projected rates of inflation over his or her lifetime.

The next step will be to select the most appropriate type of policy or policies to provide this coverage. Basically, there are two types of life insurance: whole life and term. However, each of these broad forms of life insurance has several dozen variations to offer as well.

Term insurance provides death benefits to designated beneficiaries during the term of the policy (usually until the insured reaches the age of 65). Generally, the premiums for term insurance are much lower than those for whole-life policies since the policies offer neither cash surrender values nor loan privileges to the policy owner. The two best known types of term insurance are level term, where the death benefit amount remains fixed throughout the term of the policy, and decreasing term, where the death benefit decreases throughout the term of the policy, as in the case of home mortgage insurance.

For most Americans under the age of 40, term insurance is a very inexpensive way to provide lump-sum cash benefits for your surviving spouse and/or dependents, to meet specific needs such as paying off a mortgage or major debts, funding your children's education, providing your beneficiaries with sufficient cash to see them through until your estate has been settled, and so forth.

Because whole-life premiums are often more expensive than term-life premiums, for years financial advisors have recommended buying term insurance and investing the difference as a practical solution to the life insurance dilemma. However, many of the newer whole-life insurance products offer a number of significant advantages that make them worth a second look.

For the most part, all whole-life policies are similar in that they usually cover the entire span of the insured's life up to age 100. They also offer the advantage of accrued cash values that may be surrendered at any point or loaned to the policyholder at interest rates that are often several percentage points lower than those available through other lending institutions. Moreover, since the annual premiums generally remain constant throughout the term of the policy, there are no dramatic increases to contend with every time you have a birthday.

Whole-life policies also offer a degree of flexibility not always available with term policies. For example, you can choose between having a lump-sum payment plan, a fixed monthly payment plan, a fixed-period payment plan, or any combination thereof.

Perhaps the most exciting insurance products to enter the marketplace in recent years are universal and variable life. Both of these policy types are similar in that the policy owner has a greater degree of control both in terms of the amount of insurance coverage he or she wishes at any particular period of time and the rate of interest his or her insurance dollars can earn throughout the life of the policy.

When a payment is made to the insurance company toward one of these policies, a certain percentage is allocated for the insurance premium while the balance and/or cash value is invested in short-term investments (universal life) or a choice of mutual funds, money market funds, or other investment vehicles (variable life). With a universal-life plan, the owner of the policy has flexibility in terms of the actual premiums paid and the face amount of the death benefits. With a variable-life plan, although the premiums and face amounts are generally fixed, the policy owner has greater flexibility regarding the type of investment media to which the cash value will be allocated. Most important of all, the interest earned through these policies remains tax-free for as long as the policy remains in force and the earnings are not withdrawn.

Your financial planner should be willing to take the time to discuss the various forms of life insurance available to you and your family as well as the advantages and limitations of each. Before making your final selection, following are a few important factors for you to consider.

1. **Flexibility.** Because your insurance needs are likely to change, make sure the policy offers you an adequate degree

of flexibility. For example, the term-life policy you select should offer conversion privileges to whole life, and whole life policies should permit you to change the face value and settlement options.

2. **Management.** Although the newer whole-life products may offer a variety of attractive investment alternatives, they may also require a greater degree of management. If you don't want to make decisions about where to invest your insurance dollars for maximum return, then a more traditional form of whole-life or term policy should be selected.

3. **Quality.** A company that pays you 3 percent more on your whole-life dollars may seem like a good investment at the time, but what good is the extra 3 percent if the company goes bankrupt or is unable to pay the funds to your beneficiaries as promised? Before you sign on the dotted line, take a good look at the insurance company itself, not just the product it is offering. There are a number of excellent resources that provide information of this type including *Best's Review, Life/Health Insurance Edition*.

4. **Beneficiaries.** Make sure you have the right to change the beneficiary of your policy at any time. Also, be sure to list a contingent beneficiary, especially if your spouse is listed as the primary beneficiary. When listing children as beneficiaries, it is much easier to state "all children of this marriage" than to try to remember to add the name of each new child to your policy as he or she is born.

5. **Policy Ownership.** The owner of the policy is the only one who has the right to change designated beneficiaries and to surrender, cancel, or borrow against the policy. Whether you list yourself or someone else as the owner of the policy may have certain tax implications as well.

Loss of Assets

Since our personal assets often represent a large percentage of our net worth, it stands to reason that we must take some active measures to protect them. Imagine how financially devastated you would be if you lost your home, your furnishings, your clothing, and your automobile in a fire and had to replace all of these items yourself. Very few people could withstand a loss of this scope, and yet far too few carry adequate insurance coverage against such a possibility.

When selecting an insurance policy for your home or automobile, there are two guiding principles that when followed will help you to get the most for your insurance dollars. First, pay as much attention to the items that are *not* covered as you do to the items that *are* covered. For example, if that old tree in your backyard falls down one windy day and crashes through the roof of your house, your policy will probably cover the roof repairs, but does it also cover the cost of buying a new tree? If a thief breaks into your home by jimmying a window and steals your television set most policies will reimburse you for the loss immediately. But what if your television set disappears and there is no sign of forced entry into your home? (Perhaps the milkman grabbed it and threw it into the back of his truck while you were rummaging upstairs for some money to pay him for the delivery.) Many policies do not cover what are known as "mysterious" disappearances, and yet such losses occur all the time. If your diamond ring is stolen out of your hotel room in New York and you have paid for additional jewelry coverage, then you can probably pick out a new one before you head for home. But what if the loss occurs while you are traveling abroad? Are you still covered when you leave the continental United States? If your living-room furniture is destroyed in a fire, your insurance policy will certainly pay up—but at what prices? Will they reimburse you at the prices you originally paid for the furniture in 1981 or will they reimburse you at "replacement cost," that is, the actual amount you would have to pay for the same sofa, tables, and lamps at today's prices?

Once you know exactly what a policy does and does not cover, then the final decision becomes easy. However, before you make that final decision, do some comparative rate shopping. Usually, you can find at least a half dozen companies that offer exactly the same coverage and yet the annual premiums for that coverage may vary by as much as $500 or $600!

When you have your valuable possessions adequately protected against theft, fire, accidents, and a few dozen other potential perils, there is still one more risk you need to consider insuring against, a risk that is just as devastating as a fire and probably twice as likely to occur in your lifetime—a lawsuit.

If you have ever wondered why your insurance premiums keep rising even though you have never had an accident or made a single claim for a loss in all the years you have owned them, the answer lies in the fact that we have become a "take-'em-to-court" society. And we don't just take people to court for a few hundred or a few thousand these days. Instead, we are after several hundred thousand or even several million to right the supposed wrong. Being sued for a million dollars might sound absurd to you, especially when your total personal assets only amount to several hundred thousand, but it can and does happen every day.

Although your homeowner's and automobile policies generally carry a few hundred thousand dollars worth of liability insurance against such possibilities, for as little as a $100 a year you can purchase an umbrella policy that will cover you for up to $1 million. With the price tag as low as it is for this type of coverage, an umbrella policy is certainly within everyone's means, and considering our current legal system, probably a form of protection that none of us can afford to be without.

How Much Is Enough?

While it is important to make sure you have adequate insurance coverage to protect your income, your heirs, and your assets, it is equally important to make sure you are not *over-insured*. Let's face it, insurance companies are in business to *make* money, not give it away. The best way for them to make money is to encourage you to carry more coverage on a particular risk than you really need or to opt for deductibles or elimination periods that are too low or too short.

Since risk management deals in future possibilities rather than current realities, it is often difficult to determine how to allot your insurance dollars most effectively. Should you put most of those dollars into life insurance or home coverage? Should you protect yourself primarily against the possibility of an appendectomy or an accident? Is your home more likely to be broken into or burned to the ground?

While a multitude of statistical data may be helpful in determining your insurance priorities, you have no way of knowing in advance whether you will have the good fortune of avoiding the 1 in 10 occurrence of Catastrophe A only to become an unfortunate victim of the one-in-a-million long shot known as Catastrophe B. With the exception of life insurance (death being the only guaranteed risk we all face) you may never need the coverage offered by all of the other policies. But, you may need them all.

Although using "the odds" to determine the allocation of your insurance dollars may sometimes be a good idea, there is a more practical way to solve this dilemma, and that is to evaluate the financial impact a particular loss would have on your overall net worth.

Example

Let's assume you have just purchased a home valued at $150,000 and your current net worth is $400,000. You are torn between the idea of insuring your home against fire for full value or lowering the annual premium by several hundred dollars by insuring only 80 percent of the value of your home. Your agent has also asked you to make a decision regarding the deductible for theft. Your choice is to go with the standard $250 deductible, increase the deductible and save an extra several hundred dollars a year in premiums, or eliminate the deductible altogether thereby increasing your annual premium by several hundred dollars.

Figure 9–1
Analysis of Impact of Covered Losses

Loss of $150,000 Home Due to Fire	
Coverage = 100% of Current Value	$150,000
Financial Impact	$0
Impact on Net Worth	0%
Loss of $150,000 Home Due to Fire	
Coverage = 80% of Current Value	$120,000
Financial Impact	$30,000
Impact on Net Worth	7.5%
Theft Loss with Zero Deductible	
Financial Impact	$0
Impact on Net Worth	0%
Theft Loss with $250 Deductible	
Financial Impact	$250
Impact on Net Worth	.062%
Theft Loss with $1,000 Deductible	
Financial Impact	$1,000
Impact on Net Worth	.25%

According to statistical data, the odds are far greater that your home will be broken into rather than burned to the ground in a fire. Consequently, your initial inclination is to take the few hundred dollars you would save by insuring only 80 percent of the value of the home against fire and use this money to reduce your theft deductible to zero. However, since the odds don't always work in our favor, Figure 9–1 considers the financial impact either of these situations would have on your net worth.

As you can see, although the odds might suggest leaning toward lower theft deductibles and lower fire coverage, the potential financial impact of either of these risks suggests just the opposite. A loss by fire would erode nearly 8 percent of the family's net worth while a theft loss of $1000 would barely affect the status quo. If you aren't a risk-taker, you would be far better to opt for 100 percent fire coverage and offset the increased cost of coverage by electing the higher theft deductible.

THE SENSE

As a wise man once observed, "Life is too unpredictable for anyone to write an autobiography in advance." The primary function of risk management, therefore, is to provide us with some measure of financial protection in a world where there simply are no guarantees. Unfortunately, there is a price to be paid for this type of security, a price which many people find excessive and objectionable. They argue that by investing the money they would have spent on insurance premiums over a 30- or 40-year span, they can achieve a measure of financial security much sooner. In other words, they prefer to play the odds and go through life hoping their number won't come up. As with all games of chance, if they are right they will win handsomely, and if they are wrong, they will lose heavily.

Since the primary purpose of personal financial planning is to create some measure of financial security for yourself and your family, the real question to be answered is not whether you should have coverage against all forms of risk, but rather how much money you should invest in the various types of insurance policies you will require to achieve this goal.

One of the advantages of working with a competent financial planner is that he or she can often help you obtain a maximum degree of coverage for a minimal annual investment. By upgrading old policies, building around existing employee benefits, raising deductibles, lengthening waiting periods, and reducing coverages in areas where you are currently over-insured, you may find your premiums more manageable and your insurance protection more attractive. However, in the end, you must be the judge and jury in the court of risk management, carefully weighing potential savings against potential losses and perceived risks against expensive premiums.

There is a story about a well meaning but overzealous insurance agent who was trying to convince his prospect to purchase an accident insurance policy. Unconvinced as to its merits, the prospect said, "I still don't see why I should pay all that money to get this policy," to which the agent replied, "Last year I sold the same policy to another man about your age. The other day he fell down some stairs and broke his neck, and my company sent him a check for $50,000. Just think," the excited salesman said, "tomorrow *you* could be the lucky one!"

Although the insurance agent's choice of words is certainly questionable, the point he is making is indeed valid—tomorrow you *could* be the one. Tomorrow it could be you driving home from work having to swerve suddenly to avoid hitting a young child who has run out into the street after a bouncing ball. Fortunately, you miss the child, but unfortunately, you smash into a telephone pole at 40 mph.

Several hours later, lying in your hospital bed, the doctor brings you the bad news. In addition to a bad concussion you have sustained multiple injuries including several cracked ribs, a bad case of whiplash, and a broken leg. To make matters worse, the X-rays indicate that there are some bone fragments in your leg that must be removed immediately before your leg bone can be set.

Finally, after several weeks in the hospital, you are well enough to hobble home on crutches. As you are checking out, however, the hospital gives you one more piece of bad news. It seems that in addition to breaking your leg you strained some ligaments, and you will require several months of physiotherapy once the cast is off in order to restore your leg to its former condition. And then, as if to add insult to injury, you are presented with the bill for your operation and your stay in the hospital.

The whole way home in the taxi (your car is still in the shop being repaired) you are shaking your head in disbelief at the size of the hospital bill. But little do you realize that this is only the beginning of your financial woes. Just as you are coming in the front door the telephone begins to ring. It is a very unpleasant lawyer calling to inform you that you are being sued for $150,000. According to the lawyer, your car struck the telephone pole with such force that the pole actually snapped in half. Unfortunately, the top half fell down on the top of someone's antique show car—and the owner happened to be in the front seat of the car at the time. In addition to paying his medical bills and lost wages, you are also going to have to pay to have the antique car fully restored.

Just when you think it can't get any worse, the mechanic calls up to tell you that for what it would cost to repair your car, you'd be far better buying a new one.

Around this time you decide that you'd better take a look at your insurance policies and find out exactly where you stand. You begin with your major medical plan and discover that you are responsible for the first $5,000 worth of medical bills and 20 percent of the balance. So far, you are about $15,000 in the hole and you haven't even begun your physiotherapy treatments yet.

Your auto insurance policy doesn't seem to help much either. Since you were trying to keep your premiums as low as possible in order to take a vacation in Jamaica this year, the liability portion of your policy leaves you $50,000 short if the antique car owner wins his lawsuit against you (which he probably will.)

By the time you have added up the total damage, not only is your trip to Jamaica out of the question for the next 20 years, but so is your son's college education, your new house, and your early retirement. Everything that you had hoped for, planned for, and dreamed about for years is over in a split second.

As remote as this scenario may seem, it could happen and in fact does happen every day. In a matter of hours or even seconds you can become financially devastated despite all your hard work and planning. That is why risk management is an important part of your personal defense against life's catastrophes. You can choose to ignore it if you wish, but sooner or later your decision will come back to haunt you.

Exercise 9–2
Working with Your Planner—Summary Checklist

Before

( ) Gather all current insurance policies for your planner to review.

( ) Identify particular areas of concern or perceived need.

( ) Establish your risk management goals, particularly in the area of life insurance.

During

( ) Ask your planner to explain why certain types of policies are being recommended.

Exercise 9–2 continued

( ) Have the planner obtain quotes on comparable policies from a variety of companies to be certain that you are getting the lowest possible premium for that particular coverage.

( ) Have your planner review all terms of each of the insurance policies with you, including perils/risks covered, exclusions, limits, deductibles, and so forth.

( ) If your planner is going to be receiving a commission if you select any of these policies, consider obtaining an outside opinion before you make your final decision.

( ) Make certain that the ownership, beneficiary designations(s), and settlement options are consistent with your estate plans.

After

( ) Once you have selected certain policies, make sure you act on your decision immediately. Do not procrastinate.

( ) Your policies should be reviewed at least every two or three years. Policies should be reviewed immediately upon changes in your personal or financial circumstances.

10
Tax Planning

THE DOLLARS

Although we tend to think of April 15 as the ultimate day of reckoning, the truth is that we are required by law to pay taxes all year long. That is why your employer withholds a certain amount of your gross paycheck for Uncle Sam and those who are self-employed, or who have substantial incomes from other sources such as stock market investments, must make quarterly payments to the IRS.

Since we pay taxes at regular intervals throughout the year, it stands to reason that tax planning should be a year-round endeavor as well. Come the 15th of April, there should be no unexpected surprises for taxpayers. If you are stunned by the staggering sums you have yet to pay or unexpectedly elated by the size of the refund you are going to receive, then obviously you have given very little attention to tax planning. Either way, this year-long negligence will cost you. If you owe the government a great deal of money, you will probably find yourself paying additional penalties, which may run as high as 20 percent. If the government owes you a hefty refund, then you are still a loser since someone else has been earning interest and enjoying the use of *your* money for a whole year!

Tax Planning Schedule

Most Americans pay far more taxes than they should for one simple reason: They have no idea where they stand with the IRS until a few hours, or at best, a few days before their tax returns are due. Unfortunately, if you haven't shifted and sheltered your income long before April rolls around, then you will have very few options available. It is too late by then to do anything but pay or pray.

Since one of the goals of personal financial planning is to get the most out of every dollar you earn, a good financial planner will want to review your tax situation at regular intervals throughout the year in order to minimize the percentage of each dollar that might otherwise be lost to excess taxation.

April

The best time to plan for the upcoming tax year is shortly after you have completed this year's tax return. Like an athlete who has just participated in a grueling marathon, you need to assess your strengths and weaknesses while the event is still fresh in your mind. Once you have analyzed your performance, you will then know exactly what changes you should make to emerge victorious when you run the same course again next year.

July

So far your tax planning has been based on last year's earnings and deductions, which is always the best place to start. Now that the first half of the year has passed, you are probably in a position to predict with greater accuracy your actual earnings and tax-deductible expenses for the current tax year. Your planner should review these new projections and assist you by making recommendations for additional steps to minimize your tax liability.

October–November

Either in late October or early November your tax situation should be reviewed carefully. December 31 is now fast approaching, and once this day has come and gone all of the possible options and opportunities to reduce your tax burden will have passed you by. By planning this in-depth review at least one or two months before year-end, you will have plenty of time to investigate and select the best methods of sheltering, shifting, or deferring taxable income. If you wait until the last week or two in December, you may find yourself making some very hasty decisions, the consequences of which could haunt you for years to come.

February–March

Don't wait until the last minute to have your tax returns prepared. After the first of the year, there may be a few things you can do to minimize your tax payments, provided you have ample time to see them through. Also, in the event that you have miscalculated or erroneously projected along the way, the sooner you find out what the bottom line is going to be the better. If you are due a refund, then you will want to mail your return as soon as possible. If you owe money to the government, an extra 30 or 60 days to determine the best way to meet those financial obligations can save you from liquidating the wrong assets or borrowing at loan-shark rates.

Although we have specified four particular times when you should meet with your personal financial planner, any time your tax situation changes during the year is the time to call a conference. The best time to consult with your planner is before you sell your home, purchase that piece of rental property, or dump those falling stocks. By spending just a few minutes with your financial planner whenever you anticipate a change in your financial situation, the difference this will make by next April 15th could be considerable. More often than not, the extra few hundred dollars you spend on consulting fees throughout the year will be returned to you in the form of several thousand dollars worth of tax savings.

Minimizing Your Tax Burden

Your current lifestyle and your future security all center around one thing: after-tax income. For this reason, whatever can be done to minimize your taxes must be given high priority in your financial affairs.

Taking whatever action you can take to reduce your tax obligations is not only perfectly legal (provided, of course, that the measures you employ fall within the legal boundaries of the current tax codes) but one of your rights as an American citizen. In the words of Judge Learned Hand, "There is nothing sinister in so arranging one's affairs as to keep taxes as low as possible."

There are literally hundreds of perfectly legitimate tax strategies most Americans can use to reduce their income tax bite. The methods your planner recommends will be entirely dependent upon your personal financial situation. While it would be impossible to discuss every form of tax deduction, credit, or exemption in this book, we can examine the basic categories from which your planner will be developing your personal tax plan.

Shifting Income

As the name implies, this strategy involves the shifting of earned income from a family member in a high tax bracket to a family member who is in a lower tax bracket. Currently a spouse, child, or other dependent relatives can earn up to $1900 a year and still be considered a dependent on your tax return. Although children who earn income will no longer be entitled to claim a personal exemption on their own tax return if their parents claim them as a dependent, the tax rate applied to a child who earned $1000 in

Figure 10–1
Comparison of Tax Rates on Interest Earned

	Parents	Child
Tax Bracket	35%	11%
Taxes due on $1,000 Earned Interest	$350	$110

interest will be considerably lower than the tax rate applied to the parents whose taxable income amounted to $60,000 that year. (See Figure 10–1.)

There are several different ways to shift income to a family member in a lower income bracket. If you own your own business, you can pay a salary to your spouse or your children. Bonds and other investment vehicles can be purchased in the name of dependents so that all earned interest will be taxed at a more favorable rate. Interest-free loans also can be made in virtually any amount to any family members, and earnings on the invested portion of that loan would be taxable to the recipient rather than the lender.

Sheltering and Deferring Income

Whenever the term "tax shelter" is mentioned, most people automatically think of some quasilegal investment offering four-to-one write-offs that are guaranteed to trigger a tax audit; and yet there is a number of ways to shelter income from taxation, ways that are perfectly legal and highly effective.

Probably the most common form of tax shelter is real estate. If your personal residence appreciates 200 percent in five years, you don't have to pay the government a nickel until you actually sell it. In fact, you don't even have to worry about paying taxes *after* you sell it provided you purchase another home of equal or greater value. A couple could conceivably begin in their early 20s with a $50,000 home and wind up owning a $500,000 home in their late 50s without every paying taxes on their gains, simply by making wise purchases and continually buying a home of equal or greater value.

Another popular tax shelter is a pension plan such as an IRA or a Keogh. Although the government sets a cap on the annual pension contributions that you can make to these plans in any tax year[1], there is absolutely no limit on the amount of tax-free

---

[1]Under the 1986 Tax Reform Act, taxpayers who are not eligible for employer-sponsored retirement benefits are still entitled to claim the full IRA deduction. If both spouses are employed, each spouse may deduct $2000 a year for an IRA contribution ($4000 per couple). If only one spouse is employed, the maximum tax-deductible contribution is $2250.

If either spouse is eligible for employer-sponsored retirement benefits, some or all of the IRA contribution may still be deductible. In the case of a two-income family, the total IRA contribution may be deducted provided the couple's adjusted gross income (before subtracting the IRA contribution) is less than $40,000. A single-income family may deduct the full IRA contribution provided the wage earner's adjusted gross income is less than $25,000.

Taxpayers who are eligible for employer-sponsored retirement benefits, and whose adjusted gross incomes equal or exceed the $40,000 or $25,000 figures, will lose approximately one dollar for every five dollars worth of adjusted gross income over these limits. However, regardless of your adjusted gross income, all taxpayers are entitled to deduct a minimum of $200 a year for their IRA contributions.

The maximum contribution to a 401(k) plan has been set at $7000 in 1987 and will be adjusted annually for inflation in subsequent tax years. In addition to reducing the maximum contribution to these retirement plans from $30,000 to only $7000 a year, the new laws also impose a 10 percent penalty on early withdrawals from the plan. Only those contributors who have reached age 59-1/2, or who have retired, died, become disabled or suffered a financial hardship will be exempt from this 10 percent penalty. With regard to the "financial hardship" exclusion, the IRS has yet to provide a clear interpretation of this term.

For Keogh plans the maximum tax-deductible cap has been set at $30,000 per annum. If you are making contributions to a Keogh plan which requires the contribution of a fixed percentage of income each year, you may contribute up to 20 percent of your net earnings from self-employment. If you are making contributions to a profit-sharing Keogh plan, i.e., a plan which allows you to vary the percentage of your contributions each year, your tax-deductible contribution limit is now 13.043 percent of net self-employment earnings. In addition, those who are contributing to Keogh plans will not be eligible to claim a deduction for IRA contributions unless their income is less than $50,000 when filing jointly or $35,000 on an individual return.

interest you can earn for as long as the money remains in the plan. Granted, the interest earnings are only sheltered until you begin to withdraw the funds. However, since you are unlikely to make any withdrawals until after you have retired, you will have earned tax-free interest on all monies in the plan during your highest tax bracket years and will be paying taxes on those earnings as you withdraw the funds in your lowest tax bracket years.

Even certain investments offer a limited form of tax shelter. A stock you purchased can double, even triple in value by age 65, and you won't be taxed on the gain until you actually sell it for a profit. Once again, the asset has appreciated in value during peak earning years and the gain can be sheltered until later in life when your annual earnings may be only a half or even a quarter of your former salary.

Before electing a program involving sheltering or deferring income there are two important points to remember. First, if you change your mind in midstream there may be substantial penalties to face in addition to the taxes. For example, if you invest in short term Treasury bills, you don't have to pay taxes on the gains until the bills actually mature. If you sell them prior to maturity, you will either have to sell them at a loss or be prepared to pay a gains tax in a year when you can least afford it. With regard to pension plans, if you aren't prepared to let your money ride until you retire, then shelter your income somewhere else. The penalties for making an early withdrawal from your IRA could be as high as 20 percent!

Second, remember that in most cases you are only sheltering your income temporarily. Sooner or later, in order to enjoy the gain, you must be prepared for the pain. In other words, if you decide to liquidate any capital gain realized from a tax-sheltered investment, you will have to pay taxes on those funds during that tax year. Whenever possible, try to shelter your income in such a way that you do not have to tap into the whole amount when all you really need is a small portion. Even at age 65, if you had to pay taxes on $150,000 worth of sheltered earnings, the tax burden could be devastating.

With regard to other forms of tax shelters, be sure you understand exactly what you are getting into before you commit yourself. Generally, the primary function of a good tax shelter is to create artificial or paper losses and expenses that can be used to lower your taxes over a long term while simultaneously creating actual profits that will be taxable only when the investment is sold or the gains are drawn off. Since most tax shelters require a fairly sizable investment, you need to examine the potential profits and inherent risks as closely as you do the tax benefits. Remember, there is only so much milk you can get from a cow and there are only so many deductions you can squeeze out of a tax shelter.[2]

Timing Income and Deductions

This is where working with a good financial advisor can really pay off. Suppose, for example, you have been offered a better paying job (an extra $10,000 a year) in another city and are planning to start work with that company in mid-January of the following year. It is now late November and you have just found a buyer for your home. Although you will be experiencing a substantial gain on the sale, you aren't concerned since you plan to buy another home of equal or greater value in December and take the moving expense deductions during the current tax year. As far as you're concerned, there is no reason to meet with your financial advisor since there doesn't appear to be a tax problem.

[2]The 1986 Tax Reform Act caused a number of sweeping changes in the structure and function of tax shelters. The most significant change was the 4-year phase-out program aimed at preventing the use of tax losses from the investment to reduce the investor's other taxable income. Congress argued that since most of these so-called losses exist only on paper (e.g., depreciation), any deductions or credits associated with such investments now can be used only to reduce or offset any income that is actually realized from the investment.

Unfortunately, you not only made a wrong decision, but a very costly error. While you may have saved yourself $50 by not making that appointment, your decision to proceed without your advisor's advice has just cost you $700 in taxes! (See Figures 10–2, 10–3, and 10–4 for the explanation.)

Figure 10–2
Deductible Relocation Expenses

Moving Expenses	$4,000
Cost to Purchase New Residence	3,000
Points/Interest on New Mortgage	3,000
Total Deductible Expenses	$10,000

Figure 10–3
Taxable Income Without Relocation Deduction

Taxable Income This Year	$45,000
Taxes Due	$8,840
Taxable Income Next Year	$55,000
Taxes Due	$12,340

Figure 10–4
Taxable Income Less Relocation Deduction

Taxable Income This Year	$45,000
Less Relocation Expenses	10,000
Total Taxable Income	$35,000
Total Taxes Due	$6,040
Total Tax Savings	$2,800
Taxable Income Next Year	$55,000
Less Relocation Expenses	10,000
Total Taxable Income	$45,000
Total Taxes Due	$8,840
Total Tax Savings	$3,500

As you can see from Figure 10–3, you would have been better off buying your house and making the move on January 1 than on December 31, since the relocation deduction would have completely offset the increased taxes due as a result of your $10,000 a year raise.

Regardless of how simple or unimportant a change in your financial situation might seem to be, it usually pays to consult with your financial planner before you make a final decision. Both the purchase and sale of real estate, stocks, bonds, and other investment media must be properly timed in order to minimize the potential impact on your tax return.

Tax-Favored Income

If you are in a relatively high tax bracket, you should be on the lookout for any solid investment that offers attractive tax advantages. Since the return on an investment is only as good as the actual dollars and cents that are yours to keep, a lower yielding tax-favored investment sometimes can be more valuable than a higher yielding instrument that is fully taxable. Tables 10–1 and 10–2 illustrate how transferring some of your investment portfo-

Table 10–1
Johnson Family Investment Portfolio

Assets/Investments	Amount Invested	Interest Rate	Annual Income
Checking Account	$ 3,000	0	$ 0
Savings Account	5,000	4	200
Certificates of Deposit	12,000	8	960
U.S. Government Bonds	3,000	8	240
2nd Mortgage	15,000	11	1,650
Total Investable Assets	$38,000		
Total Annual Income (before taxes)		8.0%	$3,050

lio into tax-favored instruments such as municipal bonds can increase your after-tax returns.

The Johnsons have approximately $38,000 worth of invested assets. At present, nearly 10 percent of their portfolio is sitting idle in a zero-interest checking account while approximately 40 percent of their assets are invested in certificates of deposit and U.S. Government bonds, both of which are scheduled to mature annually. Another 40 percent of their portfolio is in a high-interest second mortgage they hold on a local piece of residential real estate.

On the surface, it would appear that the Johnsons are getting a fairly good return on their investments. However, by the time you factor in the current rate of inflation (6 percent) and the taxes due on their combined incomes and investment earnings (22 percent) the Johnsons are actually increasing their net worth by only $99 a year. (Figure 10–5)

Table 10–2 shows how, after a few hours with a financial planner who recommended some practical alternatives, the Johnson's financial picture changed.

Table 10–2
Johnson Family Investment Portfolio—Revised

Assets/Investments	Amount Invested	Interest Rate	Annual Income
Checking Account	$ 600	0	$ 0
Money Market Account	2,400	6	144
30-Day Certificates of Deposit	5,000	6.5	325
Keogh Plan (Mutual Funds)	5,000	8	400 *
Municipal Bonds	8,000	5	400 *
Rental Property	17,000	7.5	1,275 *
Total Investable Assets	$38,000		
Total Annual Income (before taxes)		6.7%	$2,544

*Tax-Free Income

Figure 10–5
Net Gain After Taxes and Inflation

Investment Income	$3,050
Impact of Inflation Erosion on Total Invested Assets	(2,280)
Income Tax on Investment Income	(671)
Net Gain on Investments	$ 99
Total Annual Increase of Net Worth	$ 99

As you can see, with the use of higher yielding money market accounts and short-term certificates of deposits, the planner was able to meet the Johnson's liquidity requirements while at the same time earning them additional interest on these funds. The planner then selected three additional instruments to allow the Johnsons to receive tax-free income and shelter their gains. The Keogh plan gives the Johnsons an additional $5000 a year deduction; and the rental property (which is appreciating at an average annual rate of 6 percent) will be depreciated on paper, not only offsetting the rental income but also providing an additional $3000 in write-offs. Since these additional deductions put the Johnsons in a much lower tax bracket (14.5 percent), even though they are earning less on their investments, they are actually profiting substantially (Figure 10–6).

By investing the same $38,000 in a variety of tax-favored and/or tax-sheltered investments, the Johnsons' portfolio has increased in value by nearly $3,800 a year—a very substantial increase for only a few hours with a competent financial advisor.

Figure 10–6
Net Gain on Revised Investment Portfolio

Investment Income:	Tax Free	$2,075
	Taxable	469
Inflation Erosion		(2280)
Income Tax on Investment Income		(68)
Net Gain on Investments		$ 196
Appreciation on Rental Property (valued at $60,000)		$3,600
Total Annual Increase of Net Worth		$3,796

THE SENSE

Since you landed your first job, the time you have spent complaining or worrying about your tax problems probably would have been sufficient to read the *Encyclopedia Britannica* from A to Z. Rather than waste another moment on the problem, you would be much further ahead to devote just a fraction of that time working on the solution. Your tax problems are never going to go away on their own. In fact, as your income and assets continue to grow in the years ahead, your tax burdens are going to become heavier and heavier unless you do something about your situation right now.

There never has been and never will be a better time than now to sit down with your financial advisor and develop a concrete plan for minimizing your tax load. The sooner you get on with it, the better off you will be financially. Suppose, for example, that by making a few minor adjustments to your investment portfolio your planner found a way to save you a few hundred dollars a year. A few hundred dollars might not seem like very much to get excited about until you consider the fact that a single dollar invested each year at 10 percent would find you nearly $165 richer in 30 years time. If your tax advisor were able to save you $200 a year, those invested tax savings could mean an extra $33,000 in your pocket by the time you retire. If he or she were able to save you $2000 a year, then start making plans right now for how you intend to spend your extra $329,000!

You see, when you procrastinate where taxes are concerned, the end result is that you cost yourself unnecessary time, headaches, and money. Taxes, like death, are entirely unavoidable. There is absolutely nothing you can do to get out of paying taxes. However, there is virtually an unlimited number of strategies that any American can use to minimize the damage. And the sooner you initiate an effective tax reduction program through year-round planning, the better your finances will be in the long run.

Compared with the rest of the world, Americans actually have it relatively easy at tax time. If you had earned $100,000 in Sweden in 1985 you would have had to pay the government nearly $86,000 in taxes! The residents of Portugal and Denmark didn't fare much better. On the same $100,000 in earned income, they would have had to fork over approximately $63,000 and $58,000, respectively.

As an American, your tax bite would have been $37,000, less than one-half what your poor Swedish counterpart paid. When you stop to consider all the advantages we enjoy as a result of our tax system, including quality schools for our children, and a standard of living that makes us the envy of millions of people around the world, there is a high rate of return on our tax dollars.

Exercise 10-1
Working with Your Planner—Summary Checklist

Before

( ) Gather copies of your federal and state tax returns for the last three years for your planner to review.

( ) Be prepared to outline your tax planning goals and the steps you have taken so far to minimize your tax burden.

During

( ) Do not sacrifice safety of principal for lower taxes. Your primary concern should be the security of your assets.

( ) Your financial planner should not only recommend tax-saving ideas, but also a plan for how to invest surplus funds to increase your net worth.

( ) If the planner recommends a particular tax shelter or tax-advantaged investment strategy from which he or she will derive a commission, this fact must be disclosed by the planner. Be sure to investigate these recommendations carefully since a degree of bias may be involved.

Exercise 10–1 continued

( ) Do not sacrifice liquidity for tax savings. Most investment instruments that offer a high degree of tax sheltering also require you to tie up your money for extended periods. Before you commit your funds to a long-term investment program, be certain you have sufficient funds in highly liquid assets to draw on in the event of cash-flow emergencies; or you may incur substantial penalties, taxes, or losses for early withdrawals.

( ) Don't be afraid to get a second opinion regarding any tax plan recommendations. It is far better to pay a few hundred dollars for a second opinion now than to pay several thousand dollars in back-taxes and penalties later.

( ) A good tax plan is a realistic plan. Be wary of anyone who promises to reduce your taxes to zero or to only 5 or 6 percent. Unless your gross income is extremely low, such promises and projections are unrealistic. Your goal should be to reduce your current tax liabilities by 5-to-10 percent. At the very most, you should try to keep your tax payments between 15 and 20 percent.

After

( ) Year-round tax planning should be included as part of the personal financial planning fee and the annual fee for the maintenance of your plan. Be sure to obtain a written statement to this effect from your planner.

( ) If you anticipate changes in your financial situation, regardless how minor or incidental they may seem, be sure to discuss these changes with your planner in advance in order to avoid any tax consequences.

11
Your Investment Portfolio

THE DOLLARS

When it comes to investments, most of us tend to rely on the advice of someone else. After all, with so many different investments to choose from (most of which are influenced by dozens of national and international economic factors) it is virtually impossible to hold down a full-time job, raise a family, manage a household, and still have time to become a self-educated investment whiz.

Your Investment Advisor

While relying on an investment advisor is not always a sure-fire practice, it certainly has a lot more going for it than throwing darts at a target marked "buy" and "sell." The key is to make sure you select the right advisor from the start.

If you were advised to undergo open heart surgery, you would certainly want to know a great deal about the man or woman who was going to be wielding the scalpel before you gave your consent for the operation. Some of the questions you might ask are: How long has this surgeon been performing this particular operation? What are the surgeon's medical qualifications? Does the surgeon have a good success rate for this kind of operation? What are the odds for and against me? In other words, if your life is going to be on the line, you want to make sure you're going to be getting the best medical attention possible.

The investment of your surplus funds is a life-changing operation, too. It should be treated just as seriously as any medical condition. Properly managed, your investment portfolio could yield for you an early retirement, a good education for your children, the achievement of your dreams, or financial security for a lifetime. In the hands of the incompetent, the results could be complete and irreversible financial devastation.

Since any financial undertaking is always a bit risky, why not give yourself the best possible chance right from the start by asking probing questions and demanding honest answers. If you are at all in doubt about the recommendations being made by your investment advisor, always seek a second opinion. By investing a few hours or even a few hundred dollars before you sign on the dotted line you may save yourself from a several-thousand-dollar headache.

Investment Objectives

An investment portfolio is only as profitable as it is practical. For example, if your primary investment objective is to generate additional current income, a portfolio consisting of long-term bonds and growth stocks may project well on paper, but will do nothing to affect your income today. By the same token, even if your portfolio produces handsome current yields, you have benefitted little if your overall taxes increase by 15 or 20 percent due to your success in the stock market.

As you can see, an investment portfolio must be designed with two objectives in mind at all times. First, it must help you to achieve your investment goals. And second, it must achieve those goals in a way compatible with all other aspects of your financial plan. A portfolio that fails to meet both of these objectives is a portfolio that has failed—regardless of its overall yields.

How To Select the Right Investments

The big mistake most people make when selecting investments is never looking any further than the bottom line. Like heat-seeking missiles they lock in on yields and returns, remaining completely oblivious to the many other significant factors associated with effective asset management. It is not at all surprising to anyone other than these investors that more often than not they self-destruct financially in the process.

While the potential profit associated with any investment is certainly an important consideration, it should never be the sole factor upon which you make your final decision. Instead, there are a number of other equally important elements involved in investment planning that also must be given proper attention.

Safety of Principal

How much you can afford to gamble will be determined by your net worth and your ability to "recuperate." For example, if you are in your late 50s and have only a few more years until retirement, you can't afford to take major risks with your nest egg. If you are in your mid-30s with several decades of earning ahead of you, you can take a few more risks, provided, of course, that you can sustain the immediate loss. If you only have a few thousand dollars to your name, the loss of even a few hundred could be temporarily devastating.

Even though you may be in a very strong financial position and capable of sustaining a major loss, it doesn't mean that you are a good candidate for a high-risk investment. Your emotional well-being is just as important as your financial condition. If taking a big chance is going to cause you to spend a major portion of your time worrying about the outcome, then it is far better to select a lower yielding investment that will let you enjoy a good night's rest.

Liquidity/Marketability

There are several reasons you might want to bail out of a particular investment. One, you might need the cash to meet an unexpected emergency. Two, if the investment value starts sinking, you certainly don't want to go down with the ship. And third, it might be advantageous to be able to swap or trade out of one investment into a higher yielding investment when market fluctuations occur.

Some investments—such as stocks—are highly liquid. You can buy and sell at will with the only expense being the broker's commissions. Other investments, such as certificates of deposit, require you to tie up your funds for a predetermined period of time and impose substantial penalties for early withdrawal. The degree of liquidity you should maintain in your portfolio will depend on a variety of factors, including cash on hand, ability to access credit, and so forth.

Ease of Management

Some people love to dabble in the stock market; others don't even care to look through the financial section of the newspaper. Some investments require you to make only one or two decisions every few years; others require you to make decisions every two or three weeks. If you enjoy being actively involved in asset management, then obviously this is a low priority consideration for you. However, if you don't want to have to give a lot of thought and time to your portfolio, then you will want to make sure that whatever investments you select require only minimal management on your part.

Personal Biases

We all have certain preconceived notions about investments. Often our judgment may be clouded by tidbits we have picked up from relatives, cocktail-party conversations, and the media. While it is not easy to overcome these biases, you should make every effort to listen objectively and to get all of the facts before selecting or rejecting a particular investment.

Hedge Against Inflation

Inflation is a problem that is here to stay, and must be given due consideration when selecting any investment. If inflation rises 7 percent and your portfolio yields only 5 percent, then you are 2 percent poorer than you were last year.

Current vs. Future Income

People choose investments for a variety of reasons. Some enjoy having an extra few hundred dollars a month at their disposal. Others select investments that will help to ensure that their retirement years truly are golden. If you are looking to your investment portfolio to assist you in meeting current cash requirements, you don't want to tie up your funds in investments that are going to take several years to mature.

Investment Capital

The amount of surplus funds you have to invest will also play a major role in determining your portfolio mix. If you have only limited funds available, many investments will simply be out of your league.

Leverage

One way to increase your investment capital is to borrow funds for that purpose. In a sense, that's exactly what we do when we buy a new home. Since we can't fund the purchase price entirely on our own, we ask the bank to make up the difference. When the real estate market is booming, it's not at all unusual for a family to borrow $100,000 from the bank at 10 percent and then realize a profit of 50 or 60 percent when they sell their residence a year or two later.

Leverage also can be used very effectively to increase your net worth in the investment arena. You could conceivably borrow several thousand dollars for six months to invest in a particular stock and realize a substantial profit even after the repayment of the principal and interest. Some investments, such as the options market or real estate ventures, operate almost entirely on leverage.

Whether you use leverage to increase your net worth will be determined by your creditworthiness and your attitude about borrowing. If you are an advocate of the "neither a borrower nor a lender be" principle, then high-leverage investments are certainly not for you.

After-Tax Return on Investments

Another important area to examine is the after-tax return or yield on each of your investments. It is easy to get lured into an investment that offers an attractive rate of return on paper, while, in practice, depending on your current tax bracket, this seemingly good deal may actually produce far less income for you than another lower yielding, tax-advantaged instrument. For example, if you are in the 30 percent tax bracket, the actual, after-tax return on an 8.5 percent tax-exempt municipal bond would be 12.14 percent. If you are in the 40 percent tax bracket,[1] that same bond would yield the equivalent of 14.17 percent!

---

[1]Author's note: Although under the Federal Tax Reform Act the highest tax bracket is 28 percent, total tax burden (including state and municipal income taxes) may be as high as 40 percent of income for certain taxpayers.

Investment Alternatives

There are literally thousands of different ways you can invest your surplus funds with dozens of new alternatives appearing on the market almost daily. Basically, each of these investments falls into one of the general investment categories described in the following section. As you will see, each has its own unique method for increasing your net worth. By the same token, each also has its own special limitations, risks, rewards, and requirements.

Real Estate

In addition to being a generally profitable venture, real estate still offers a number of major tax advantages to property owners. First, even though your property may be appreciating in value annually, you can deduct up to $25,000[2] a year in losses from repairs, improvements and/or depreciation. Second, by pooling your resources with others to form a limited partnership, you may be entitled to a percentage of losses provided your ownership share is not less than 10 percent. Third, if you don't want to play the role of landlord, repairman and rent collector, you can always hire someone else to manage the property for you while you make management decisions. And finally, real estate can also offer you a source of current income from the rents you collect.

The major drawback to real estate is that it is not always easy to liquidate your assets if you need to sell in a hurry. Moreover, if you do experience a capital gain on your property and don't purchase a similar property of equal or greater value within two years, you will be subject to tax on the profits you made on that sale. If the property is heavily depreciated, that could add up to a sizable tax problem.

[2]If your adjusted gross income exceeds $100,000, the maximum annual losses are reduced by 50 cents for each dollar your income exceeds $100,000 under the 1986 tax code amendments.

Stocks and Mutual Funds

Winning in the stock market requires a unique combination of knowledge and timing. It is not only a matter of knowing which stocks to purchase, but also when to buy and sell them.

In selecting a particular stock, there are two critical elements to be analyzed. First and foremost is the company itself. A company that offers a strong balance sheet and that is involved in a stable or growing industry is generally a good bet. However, you must also take into consideration the timing element by analyzing past stock prices and performance. The stock may have reached its peak or may be selling too high for the dividends it offers.

One of the keys to success in the stock market is diversification. By investing in a number of different stocks, you can usually minimize your losses and maximize your profits. Unfortunately, such a program is not always possible for the smaller investor who has only a limited amount of funds for this purpose. However, the same effect can be achieved by investing in mutual funds.

Basically, a mutual fund company pools the funds of all its investors and invests those funds in dozens or even hundreds of different stocks. When you purchase shares from a mutual fund company, in essence the performance of your mutual fund stock will be tied into the performance of the company's total stock portfolio. If the company's portfolio managers make the right investment decisions, the return on your shares will rise. If the company makes a series of poor investment decisions, the return and value of your shares will decrease. Consequently, you will want to investigate the track record of any mutual funds company very carefully.

You can choose among dozens of mutual fund companies depending on your specific needs and preferences. Some companies specialize in growth stocks, common stocks, or corporate bonds while others invest solely in municipal bonds or money market instruments. Some even specialize according to a particular industry, such as energy or computer technology.

Regardless which type of fund you choose, make sure you understand its load policies before you become one of its investors. The term "load" refers to a fixed commission charged by a fund to its investors when shares are purchased and/or when shares are sold. Some companies have no or very minimal load charges while others assess such high sales fees that an investor would be wise to stay clear of such unprofitable situations.

Bonds

Essentially, when you purchase a bond from either a corporation or a government agency, the certificate you get in return is a form of IOU. The issuer of the bond promises to pay you a specific amount of interest for a predetermined period of time and then to repay you the principal amount when the "loan" expires.

Obviously, a promissory note is only as good as the company that issues it. If the issuer of the bond goes bankrupt, the only value your bond will have is that of the paper it was printed on. For this reason, it is important to know as much as you can about the financial strength of the company or municipal agency offering the bond.

The major advantage offered by bonds is that the issuer of the bond has to pay you interest regardless of whether it earned any profit during the period you hold the bond. In the stock market, you only earn a profit if the company that issued the stock earns a profit. The other major advantage to bonds is that in the event the issuer should declare bankruptcy, bondholders have a prior claim against any properties, assets, or income of the issuer, which by law must be met before the claims of the stockholders are met.

Bonds also have a very active secondary market where various issues can be bought, traded, swapped or sold at discount off par (i.e., the going rate). When you buy a bond at discount the obvious profit is the difference between what you paid for it and the face value at which you will eventually redeem it. Depending on the number of years to maturity and the discount at which you purchase the bond, discounted bonds can also be a very profitable addition to your investment portfolio.

Money Market Instruments

The most common investments in this category are probably certificates of deposit and Treasury bills. Although the yield on these investments is only moderate, if safety of principal and ease of management are among your primary considerations, then the money market is generally a good safe bet.

Futures Contracts and Options

If you can live with the inherent risks and you don't mind hedging your bets with leverage, futures contracts and options can be a very rewarding investment.

Futures contracts are essentially a method of "hedging" or protecting certain assets against the risk of price fluctuations. Originally, these contracts were applied to commodities such as grains, livestocks, wood, metals, and so forth. In the last decade, this technique has been expanded to encompass various marketable securities such as certificates of deposit and Treasury bills as well as the stock market index itself.

From an investment point of view, futures contracts can also be purchased speculatively. If you predict various market fluctuations accurately, you can realize a considerable profit.

One of the major advantages of futures contracts is that these investments are highly leveraged. Consequently, an investor may only need to invest a minimal margin deposit of approximately $1000 to $2000 per contract. Maintenance margins are then determined on a daily basis depending on price fluctuations in the market. Any profits are credited to your margin account and may be withdrawn as needed. Any losses will require you to make additional deposits to your margin account to make up the difference.

When you buy a futures contract you are taking what is known as a "long position." In other words, you are buying in at a certain rate in anticipation of an increase in prices. When you anticipate that prices are going to fall, you sell a futures contract or take a "short position."

Futures options are very similar to contracts with one major difference: Your losses cannot exceed the amount of your initial investment. If your futures contracts take a swing in the wrong direction, you must pay the difference into your margin account on a daily basis. If your futures options go up or down unexpectedly and you exercise your option to buy or sell, the most you can lose is the initial deposit you paid for your option. For example, if you paid $2000 to take a particular position in the option market and prices fall $5000, the maximum amount you will lose is your $2000.

Collectibles

As the name implies, this form of investment involves a variety of items that can be collected such as rare coins, antiques, paintings, sculptures, stamps, and so forth.

Collectibles are a unique investment because they offer two different forms of income to the investor. First, assuming the items appreciate in value over a period of time, collectibles can be sold at a profit. Since the profit on these investments is only taxable when the item changes hands (either through sale or inheritance) collectibles are an excellent form of tax shelter.

The second form of income that can be derived is "psychic income." Often, those who collect such rarities do so out of the joy of ownership rather than in response to a profit motive.

Obviously, collectibles have two major drawbacks, specifically management and liquidity. Insurance premiums on works of art or rare coin collections can be astronomical. And too, there is no guarantee that you can find a buyer for your lithograph or your one-of-a-kind stamp when you need one.

Precious Metals

Investment experts offer widely varying interpretations of what is going to happen in the precious metals market. Some predict that gold is going to rise again dramatically. Others predict that an increase such as the one seen in the early 1980s is not likely to happen again for a long, long time. In any event, one thing most experts do agree on is that if you are looking for a long-term growth investment, some percentage of your portfolio should be invested in the precious metals market. However, if you are looking for current income or a hedge against inflation, you would be better investing your dollars elsewhere.

Oil and Gas Ventures

Oil and gas ventures were one of the most common forms of tax shelter prior to the recent tax revisions. Basically, an investor in an oil or gas drilling partnership was required to put up a certain sum of money and in exchange was entitled to the tax losses associated with the venture, including operating costs and depletion. In addition to the tax benefits, an investor was also taking a highly speculative but potentially lucrative position in the hope that oil or gas really would be found, in which case he or she would own a percentage of the profits. At the very least, an investor would lose only his or her initial investment, and in exchange receive some very attractive tax write-offs that would more than compensate for the investment loss.

When the new tax laws were introduced in 1986, one major change came into effect to make these partnerships less attractive. Instead of being able to take a passive role in the partnership, investors are now required to assume a "working interest." Under these rules, if the partnership needs additional funds to cover drilling expenses or losses, the partners are required to supply the additional working capital. Moreover, if something unforeseen should arise, such as a major fire or an explosion where workers are killed or severely injured, the investors themselves could be financially liable for damages not covered by the insurance policy.

Because of their tax advantages and potential for high returns, gas and oil ventures certainly should not be ignored by investors. However, greater caution must be exercised now before electing to participate in such a partnership.

THE SENSE

The perfect investment has yet to be invented. In all likelihood, there never will be one specific stock, bond, real estate venture or collectible item that will meet all your personal and financial requirements. The investment that offers the high yield you are looking for often carries an equally high element of risk. Rental property may be the perfect choice for your tax and investment specifications, but it also requires more personal time than you may care to spend right now. Those growth stocks may look promising, but what if they don't perform as expected in 10 years?

Diversification

When it comes to investments, the only way to achieve the best of all worlds is to diversify your portfolio. Only by selecting a wider variety of investment instruments can you realistically expect to achieve results. For example, the risks associated with high-yielding investments can be offset by selecting a few with lower yields and lower risk. The potential impact of those investments whose gains are fully taxable can be minimized by selecting those offering certain tax advantages.

One of the factors many experts recommend as a general guide for determining the right mixture of investments for your portfolio is your current age. Figure 11–1 depicts how, when you are in

Figure 11–1
Possible Investment Portfolio Mix Based on Current Age

Age	Liquidity	Long-Term Growth	Current Income	Hedge Against Inflation
20s	40–55%	15–30%	15–25%	0–10%
30s	10–25%	60–85%	5–15%	10–15%
40s	5–15%	70–90%	5–10%	10–15%
50s	5–15%	50–70%	5–10%	15–20%
60s	15–30%	20–40%	15–30%	5–15%

your 20s, you are in the middle of a period of relatively high consumption. This is the time when you are usually buying your first home, furnishings, a car, and so forth. Consequently, your need for liquidity and current income is significantly higher than for those in their mid-40s whose consumption rate is much lower.

Whether your primary investment goal centers around current income, a retirement nest egg, or sheltering your earnings from taxation, your best course of action is to diversify your portfolio.* Remember, too, that diversification should apply not only to specific categories of investments, but also the investments within each of those categories. For example, if 50 percent of your portfolio consists of growth stocks, then make sure you hedge your bets by selecting a variety of stocks rather than gambling on only one. Like placing a bet at the race track, you can

---

*Author's note: The importance of portfolio diversification was clearly demonstrated once again on October 19, 1987. In addition to striking a crippling blow to the assets of hundreds of thousands of private investors, the stock market crash of "Black Monday" also devastated hundreds of businesses and financial institutions.

improve your odds by spreading your money over several possible winners rather than laying it all down on one long-shot. Granted, if the long-shot pays off, you will win handsomely; but if it doesn't, you will have lost it all.

One final but very important point for your consideration: Do not under any circumstances allow yourself to become an investor through intimidation. With the recent changes to the tax codes and the seemingly endless proliferation of investment alternatives to choose from, it is easy to become overwhelmed by the whole investment process. And it is far too easy to become intimidated by someone who seems to be far more knowledgeable than yourself about the subject. When these self-appointed experts start spouting off about stock options, CATS and TIGRS, Fannie Maes, P/E ratios and the like, there is a tendency to feel like a first grader just learning to count to 10 who suddenly finds himself sitting in the middle of a college-level economics course.

More often than not, when confronted by someone who appears to be highly knowledgeable in a particular field, we will sit quietly and nod our heads sagely as though we are following every word with total comprehension. As the saying goes, "Pride goeth before a fall"; and if you let your pride stand between you and your investment advisor, you may indeed fall and fall heavily.

Never be afraid of appearing ill informed or ignorant in front of your financial planner. If you were a financial wizard, you would not need the planner's services in the first place, and an important part of your planner's job is to develop a plan that is not only comprehensive but comprehensible. If you don't understand why Stock A is better than Stock B—ask! If you don't understand the specific mechanics of a mutual fund—ask! And if you don't understand—thoroughly understand—the inherent benefits and risks of each and every recommended investment—ASK! ASK! ASK! Ultimately, losing face is preferable to losing your shirt.

Exercise 11–1
Working with Your Financial Planner—Summary Checklist

Before

( ) Develop your list of investment objectives. Be sure to prioritize the items on the list.

( ) Be clear in your own mind regarding the extent to which you are prepared to risk some or all of your assets in exchange for high profits.

( ) Prepare a complete list of all of your current investments.

During

( ) Is your investment portfolio sufficiently diversified?

- ( ) High yield/low yield
- ( ) High risk/low risk
- ( ) Taxable/tax-advantaged
- ( ) Current income/future income
- ( ) Current yield/future yield
- ( ) Liquidity/long-term growth

( ) Is your portfolio sufficiently diversified with regard to the types or categories of investments being recommended?

( ) Is your portfolio consistent with your personal financial objectives?

( ) Is your portfolio consistent with your attitude toward risk?

( ) Does your portfolio provide you with sufficient liquidity?

Exercise 11–1 continued

( ) Does your portfolio meet your requirements regarding:

- ( ) the management of your investments?
- ( ) after-tax yield?
- ( ) current income?
- ( ) future income?
- ( ) hedge against inflation?

( ) Do you have a complete understanding of all the investments in your portfolio as well as their projected rates of return, tax benefits, advantages, risks, and so on?

( ) Are you comfortable with the amount of money you are being asked to invest?

( ) Have you thoroughly investigated the competence of your investment advisor?

( ) Have you considered the advisability of getting a second opinion?

After

( ) Timing is a critical factor where investments are concerned. Be careful to implement the recommendations of your plan in a timely manner.

( ) Review the status of your investments at least once every three months.

( ) If you are dissatisfied with the results of any or all of your investments, have a meeting with your planner to discuss alternatives.

12
Retirement Planning

THE DOLLARS

Americans today are saving considerably less and spending significantly more than any other generation before them. In 1986, for example, the average amount saved by most American families was less than 4 percent of all after tax-income. Whether this alarming tendency is the result of consumer credit that encourages us to buy now and pay later, or whether we simply have been lulled into a false sense of financial security because of our relative affluence is difficult to say. In either event, a dark cloud certainly looms ahead for far too many of us.

According to statistics released by the U.S. Department of Commerce, those "golden years" we all dream about are more likely to turn out to be badly tarnished brass. Rather than living out our retirement in well deserved ease and comfort, more than 73 percent of us will be trying to figure out how to make ends meet on our meager Social Security and pension checks, supplemented by occasional handouts from our children. Another 22 percent of our generation will never retire. Instead, we will be forced by rising inflation to work, either full-time or part-time, until the day we die. Only a small handful—fewer than 5 percent—will be able to live out the remainder of their years in the physical and psychological comfort that can be achieved only through some measure of financial independence.

If the vision of being dependent on the government, an employer, or worse still, your children for meager monthly handouts after all of your years of hard work and long hours in the marketplace is not quite what you have in mind when you think of retirement, then you cannot afford to let another day go by without initiating some very specific plan to secure your future. Don't make the costly mistake of becoming so wrapped up in the daily demands of the marketplace that you seldom, if ever, pause long enough to consider exactly where your actions are leading you. Fortunately, this is one area where your financial planner can be worth his or her weight in gold. Through the financial planning process he or she will help you pause long enough to put the effort you are expending and the dollars you are earning into some kind of practical perspective that can and will serve you into your retirement years.

Developing Your Perspective

Retirement planning, like all other aspects of your financial plan, must begin with specific personal objectives. For most of us, this presents an immediate problem. It is hard to picture our lives two or three decades into the future. At age 35 we are more likely centering our thoughts around career advancement or raising a young family rather than pondering what life might hold in store for us when our children have left the nest and we have been presented the proverbial gold watch for our years of service.

Compared to the demands we are currently facing, retirement planning understandably falls by the wayside. "Johnny needs braces. The transmission has to be replaced. The roof leaks during heavy rainstorms. I've simply got to have a new suit for that meeting in St. Louis next month." These are the very real financial concerns of today. And since we have little more than a vague notion of the future, is it any wonder we respond to the concerns of the moment instead?

It has been said there are only two things in life that can make a human being take positive action: inspiration and desperation. Where retirement planning is concerned, both of these emotions can be used to achieve the same satisfactory results. In some cases, we can become sufficiently inspired by a vision of the future to give retirement planning a high priority in our lives. The investment broker who dreams of sailing around the world before his 50th birthday and the account executive who lives for the day when she can retire and try her hand at writing a best-selling novel have no difficulty finding the necessary time or money to invest in their future. They willingly sacrifice new cars and new clothes and expensive vacations because their dreams hold more attraction for them than anything the current moment has to offer.

But such people are the rare exceptions in our society. The majority of us have no burning desires or powerful dreams to inspire us. When placed side by side, our present wants seem so real and our future wishes so nebulous that the former totally obscures the latter from sight. Since inspiration isn't the answer, then desperation must be. And how we experience desperation is entirely in our hands—as a future possibility or as a future reality.

Anticipating Your Financial Needs

Imagine, for a moment, what it would be like to be a member of the 95 percent club—those retirees who failed to plan for their future financial independence. Imagine sitting anxiously by the window waiting for the postman to bring your pension check. Imagine, after devoting nearly 40 years of your life to your employers, what it must be like to have to plan your weekly meals around supermarket specials or manufacturers' coupons. Imagine how humiliating it would be to have to ask your son-in-law for money because you can't afford to repair the roof on your 30-year-old house. Imagine planning your life around the television schedule because that's the only entertainment you can afford. If all of *that* doesn't bother you, then imagine living in a one-bedroom apartment in the poorest neighborhood in your city simply because inflation has outpaced your retirement dollars and that's the only shelter you can afford.

Even though you haven't developed any concrete retirement plans yet, surely those images weren't going to be among them. And yet, that may be exactly where you are headed with your hit-and-miss savings program. Having read these words, if you find yourself thinking, "No, not me. That could never happen to me," then may we suggest that you turn once again to Exercise 4–3 in Chapter 4. Then, in Exercise 12–1 below, write your current net worth. Divide that figure by the number of years you have been employed on a full-time basis. This will give you the average amount by which you have been able to increase your net worth on an annual basis. For example, if your current net worth is $100,000 and you have been working for 10 years, your average annual increase would be approximately $10,000 a year.

Next, on the first line in Exercise 12–2, write the number of years you anticipate working on a full-time basis before you retire. Then multiply this number by the average annual increase in your net worth and add this amount to your current net worth.

Exercise 12–1
Computing Future Net Worth—Part I

Current Net Worth	$__________
Number of Years of Full-Time Employment	__________
Average Annual Increase	$__________

Exercise 12–2
Computing Future Net Worth—Part II

Estimated Years of Employment	________
Average Annual Increase	$________
Current Net Worth	$________
Estimated Net Worth at Retirement	$________

Assuming that your income continues to keep pace with inflation and that your spending, investing and/or savings habits remain as they have been over the last few years, the figure you obtain from this calculation will be approximately equal to your total net worth at the time of retirement. For example, if your current net worth is $100,000 and you anticipate another 30 years of full-time employment with an average annual increase of $10,000, then by the time you retire your net worth would be approximately $400,000 (30 X $10,000 = $300,000 + $100,000 = $400,000).

Even if the bottom line doesn't look too scary at this point, there remains a number of additional factors to take into consideration—primarily inflation. Just to give you an idea of how inflation can erode the buying power of your dollars, if you earned approximately $25,000 in 1970 you would have needed nearly $60,000 in 1980 just to maintain the same lifestyle. Had inflation increased at the same pace in the 1980s as it did in the 1970s (approximately 113 percent), you would need nearly $150,000 per year in 1990 to maintain your 1980 standard of living. In other words, even though the bottom line of your estimated net worth suggests a very comfortable lifestyle, that lifestyle could only be maintained at today's prices. In 30 years' time, you may need 10 to 15 times that amount just to avoid the poverty line!

And if you think this is nothing more than idle speculation, then just look at how prices have changed in your lifetime.

Whatever happened to the candy bar you used to buy for a nickel? What is the current value of that house your parents bought for $5000 40 years ago? How much did you pay for your first car versus the car you purchased this year? And if you think you've seen the worst of it, think again. We may have slowed down to single-digit inflation, but each one of those single digits year after year is going to keep adding to the cost of living you will have to cover with your retirement income. Feeling sufficiently desperate yet to take retirement planning seriously?

Developing Your Retirement Plan

Fortunately, it is never too late to take retirement planning seriously. In fact, the sooner you do, the better you will fare. Tables 12–1 and 12–2 show what a difference a head start can make to your retirement plans.

Table 12–1
Retirement Funds

Depositing $2000 Per Year into an IRA or Keogh Account*	
Number of Years Deposits Are Made	**Aproximate Value of Retirement Funds**
5	$ 13,616
10	36,018
15	72,875
20	133,516
25	233,288
30	397,441
35	667,520
40	1,111,878
45	1,842,973

*Assuming a 10% annual rate.

Table 12–2
Retirement Funds

Annual Deposit Required to Create $1,000,000 in Retirement Funds*

Number of Years Deposits Are Made	Approximate Annual Deposit Required
5	$148,000
10	57,000
15	29,000
20	16,000
25	9,200
30	5,500
35	3,300
40	2,000
45	1,100

*Assuming a 10% annual rate.

Whether you have some very specific retirement objectives in mind or just a general sense of the standard of living you hope to enjoy, your planner will work with you in an effort to see that these objectives are met satisfactorily. Remember, however, that if you have let things slide for too long or if you are unwilling to make the necessary financial investment in your better future, there is only so much your planner will be able to do for you. Financial planners are not miracle workers. Rather, they are skilled financial tacticians who will do the best they can with the funds you give them to work with.

One of the first things the planner will try to estimate is the approximate income you will require to maintain a particular standard of living during your retirement years. This income must be sufficient to cover all living expenses with necessary inflation adjustments.

For the most part, your living expenses during your retirement years will be considerably less than during your earning years.

With the children away from home and with the elimination of those expenses associated with earning a living such as business luncheons, weekly transportation expenses, frequent additions to your business wardrobe, and so forth, your financial needs will probably be 20-to-30 percent lower than they were when you were spending 40 hours a week or more in the marketplace and raising a family. Also, assuming you will have been living in the same home for many years, the mortgage on your family residence will probably be paid in full or low enough to refinance, further reducing your monthly overhead.

By the same token, some of your current living expenses may rise dramatically. For example, medical and dental insurance premiums now may be coming out of your personal budget rather than your employer's health care budget. If your employer supplied you with a car, then you will either have to use public transportation or take on the additional expenses of car payments, insurance, gas, and repairs. If your retirement plans include a considerable amount of travel or special recreational activities, these too have a cost factor that must be calculated into your estimated monthly living expenses.

Once your planner has developed a picture of your estimated financial requirements, the next step will be to determine the extent to which your current retirement plans and investments will meet those needs. All sources of potential retirement income, including IRAs, company pensions, Social Security, insurance annuities, and investments will be subtracted from your estimated living expenses to determine the gap between what you will require and what you will be receiving. Then your planner will focus on the development of a plan to create the necessary funds to offset that difference.

In some instances, the planner may recommend various additions to your investment portfolio, such as long-term growth stocks. In other cases, the recommendation may include increased contributions to various retirement funds. In either event, whether or not you implement these recommendations in a timely, consistent, and disciplined fashion will be entirely in your hands. As the saying goes, "You can lead a horse to water, but you can't make him drink." In financial planning terms this adage could read, "You can show a client how to enjoy a comfortable and secure retirement, but you can't make him save for it."

Because so much is riding on the advice your planner gives you, great caution should be exercised before you commit to any retirement program. Will Rogers, in response to his interest and concern about the safety of an investment, was quoted as saying, "I care far more about the return *of* my principal than I do about the return *on* my principal." That's a good philosophy for anyone to ponder. You can't afford to take risks with your future nest egg. It is far better to select an investment program or retirement fund that offers a lower return on your principal than to risk your future security on a long shot.

THE SENSE

A successful retirement involves a great deal more than financial preparation. It requires a considerable amount of psychological preparation as well.

Many years ago a prominent psychologist, Abraham Maslow, developed a theory regarding human personality that centered around the concept of basic needs. According to Maslow, man must continually experience a certain measure of comfort in each of these areas before he can be truly happy and fulfilled. Failure at any of the lower levels in the pyramid pictured in Figure 12–1 will become an obstacle to the achievement of the higher levels. Failure to achieve the higher levels will result in a human being who is endlessly frustrated and continually dissatisfied with his or her own existence.

As you can see, the most basic needs that must be met relate to our sense of physical comfort. When you are constantly struggling to come up with enough money to pay for your next meal

Figure 12–1
Maslow's Hierarchy of Human Needs

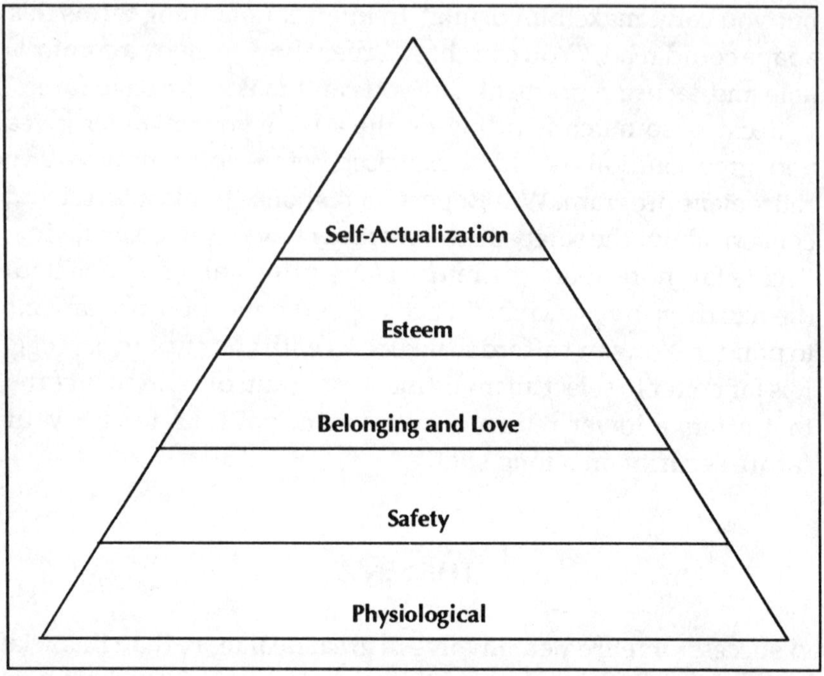

or a new pair of shoes, it's hard to imagine how you could also feel satisfied with your life.

The next level has to do with the human need for security and "maintaining the status quo." We all need the comfort of living in a community where law and order abides and where we feel at home. We also need the security of knowing that we aren't going to be evicted from our house because we couldn't meet the monthly payment. Human beings are creatures of habit, not change, and we all derive a certain sense of comfort from things that are familiar, known, predictable. Although we all enjoy surprises, most would gladly trade in 10 surprises for one simple guarantee.

Obviously, in order to satisfy these two basic needs in our

society a certain measure of financial security is required. That is why your principal concern in the area of retirement planning must be the dollars; but that should never be your only area of concern. As indicated by Maslow's diagram, there are other equally important needs that must also be considered, needs that cannot be met with a credit card or personal check.

Once we have satisfied our fundamental physical requirements we eventually focus on the higher levels of human existence—namely our social, emotional and psychological well-being. According to Maslow, the next basic need that is shared by all human beings is the need to feel a sense of belonging and love. This is a need that must be "planned" for as carefully as you plan your investment portfolio and your pension plans.

One of the things that takes most retirees by surprise is the sense of loneliness that often ensues shortly after their last day at the office. Over the years, many of the friendships and associations we develop center around our involvement in the marketplace. We go bowling with the "guys from the office." We dine out with coworkers. We associate with others who are members of the same management team, board of directors, professional associations, sales staff, or department. When we are away from the office, we interact with our growing children, participating in family events, or socializing with parents of our children's playmates.

Suddenly, all of this daily "belonging" comes to a halt. We seldom see former business colleagues because we no longer share the business-oriented bond that held us together. The people we ate lunch with at the office are now eating lunch with the person who filled our position when we retired. Our children are off to college, getting married, or busy raising a family of their own. Everything and everyone who for so many years gave us a sense of belonging and emotional security has disappeared, leaving a noticeable void in our lives.

An important part of the retirement planning process must be the discovery of a means to fill this void. Long before retirement you should be cultivating friendships and social contacts based on personal relationships rather than business affiliations or family ties. Many people find great satisfaction in participating in community projects or offering their services to fund-raising organizations. A sense of belonging can also come from joining clubs based upon common personal interests such as golfing, stamp collecting, opera, or rare books.

Whatever you think might work to satisfy your needs to feel "a part of," it is never too early to develop the contacts or explore the possibilities. By the time you retire, these outside social activities should be well established in your life so that there will be no lonely transition period to experience as you shift social gears.

Next on the list of needs are those emotions revolving around self-respect and personal achievement. Everyone needs to feel good about themselves and what they are doing. Unfortunately, after 40 years in the marketplace we have learned to rely solely on our professional achievements to provide us with a sense of own self-worth or as a yardstick by which to measure our relative success. Is it any wonder, then, that many retirees suddenly view themselves as worthless and their lives as failures? Day after day they sit analyzing all that they could have done or should have done, dragging their psyche further and further down in the process.

What it is that gives us a sense of value, of self-respect, of accomplishment? In a nutshell—purpose. Something to get out of bed for. Something to strive toward. Something to achieve. Without a sense of purpose to give meaning to our lives on a daily basis we inevitably find ourselves sleeping later in the morning, reading the newspaper from cover to cover, watching television shows from dawn until dusk, or spending time with people we don't even care to associate with. Instead of a sense of anticipation, we face each new day with a sense of dread, wondering how we are going to fill the long hours one more time.

In preparation for your years of retirement your plan should also include a new and purposeful direction. Retirement counselors often suggest that instead of thinking of this stage of your life as an ending, you should regard it as a new beginning.

Fortunately, we have all gone through those kinds of endings and beginnings many times before in our lives. When we retired from high school, we turned our attention to college. After three or four years that institution of learning also retired us with a diploma, so we focused instead on beginning a career. Throughout the next stage of our lives, we ended and began several jobs with various employers. Some us even ended and began several relationships and marriages. In the final analysis, we are all experts at closing old doors and opening new ones. Consequently, making the transition from a career to retirement should be relatively easy for us provided we give ample consideration to the particular new door (or doors) we intend to open when the door on current careers has finally closed forever.

Whatever it is that would give you a sense of purpose, of self-respect, of achievement, of long-range vision, you cannot afford to wait until after you have retired to work out the details of a meaningful plan for the balance of your life. Instead, you should begin thinking seriously in those terms at least five years before you retire. The better prepared you are mentally, emotionally, socially, and financially to make this transition, the easier and more enjoyable your retirement years will be.

The final step on the ladder of human needs is one called self-actualization. Self-actualization refers to the highest accomplishment we can achieve as human beings, specifically the realization of our own unique potential. In a way, retirement provides us with a rare gift of unlimited time and personal freedom. No longer chained to a desk or burdened with the pressures of daily appointments and professional responsibilities, we are granted a unique opportunity to travel new avenues of life that hitherto were closed to us. We can leisurely expand all the latent skills and talents that so often went ignored or unheeded during our youth simply because something else demanded our time and attention. What an incredible opportunity to learn new skills, read the classics, dabble with oil painting, stroll along a beach, savor a beautiful sunset, or perhaps even write a poem about it as we finally experience all of the best that life has to offer and all the best that we have to offer to life.

Retirement truly can be the golden pinnacle of human existence for every man and woman. But only those who have planned for it, prepared for it, and perhaps even sacrificed for it, will be the recipients of its many blessings.

Granted, there is a certain element of risk in retirement planning. There is always the chance that unforeseen circumstances will prevail. But the proponents of the "live for today" philosophy are just as in error as those whose guiding principal is "Someday . . . " Life should be a careful blending of both the present and the future, tempered by the experiences of the past. Fortunately, if you start the planning process now, future security can be gained without making major changes to your current lifestyle. In fact, most experts agree that merely by regularly saving approximately 10 percent of your gross income you can enjoy the best of both worlds. The key is to make the commitment to begin now to prepare for your future. Maybe the odds won't work out in your favor. Maybe you will never live to see retirement or to enjoy your years in the sun. But then again, what if you do?

Exercise 12–3
Working with Your Planner—Summary Checklist

Before

( ) Develop a set of clearly defined personal retirement goals or retirement lifestyle goals.

( ) If you do not have a clear picture of where, how and when you want to retire, then think in terms of what you do *not* want to experience or the minimal standard of living you would find acceptable.

Exercise 12–3 continued

( ) Gather together the data pertaining to your current retirement or pension funds.

( ) Be sure to discuss retirement with your spouse in order to develop a plan consistent with your individual as well as your shared objectives.

During

( ) Do not take risks with your nest egg. It is far better to earn less on your principal than to lose your principal.

( ) Be certain you understand all of the terms and conditions of any retirement fund, including penalties for early withdrawal, methods of withdrawal, tax consequences, and so forth.

( ) Investigate the financial stability of any financial institution or company to be certain your savings will be there when you are ready for them.

After

( ) If you do not have the discipline to save, then make the necessary arrangements to have the amounts deposited or deducted automatically.

( ) Be sure to plan your retirement hours as carefully as you plan your retirement income.

( ) Begin to develop outside social contacts and interests (i.e., non-work related).

( ) If your personal retirement plans change, make sure your financial plan reflects those changes. At the very least, you should review your objectives and your plans every two or three years.

13
Estate Planning

THE DOLLARS

On the subject of death, comedian Woody Allen once commented, "I'm not afraid to die. I just don't want to be there when it happens." As amusing as this might be, it also helps to explain the reason more people don't take estate planning seriously.

Although most people accept death as inevitable, few really like to concede their own mortality. And in a sense, that is exactly what we are doing when we make a will, create a trust, or give serious thought to the disposition of our assets. By those very acts we are admitting—finally and irrevocably—that we aren't going to be around forever. Perhaps one of the major reasons people don't plan their affairs more diligently is that, subconsciously, they are holding on to the hope that if they don't give much thought or attention to the idea, perhaps death won't give much thought or attention to them. As comforting as this theory might be, the harsh truth is that no one has yet been able to avoid the end of human existence. As the saying goes, "The only thing you can count on in life is that you aren't going to get out of it alive."

In addition to the fact that estate planning is certainly not the most pleasant project to undertake, it can also be a very expensive and confusing process. Short of buying one of those do-it-yourself will kits, your only alternative is to hire an expert to help you put your affairs in order; and, as we all know, expert advice doesn't come cheap. But if you really care about your family, sooner or later you are going to have to bite the bullet and get the job done. After all, if you think the bill for arranging your affairs is high, wait until you see the price your family will pay if you don't.

If you don't plan the disposition of your estate, the probate courts will. They will determine how your assets are to be divided among your surviving heirs. They will appoint guardians for your minor children and determine what portion of your estate should be allocated to their support. They will appoint the executors, the trustees, and the administrators; and they will extract a hefty sum for these compulsory services from your assets. You may not agree with these intestacy laws, but you aren't going to be around to do anything about it by that time. The only way to avoid these unpleasant consequences is to take steps now to assure *you* rather than some unknown *they* make the necessary decisions to provide for your loved ones in a way that reflects your personal wishes.

Regardless of the size of your estate, it is worth taking the time to plan for its proper disposition. Estate planning isn't just for the very wealthy. Far more important than the value of your assets is the value you place on the welfare of the people in your life who are depending on you to provide them with some measure of security and well-being.

Objectives of Estate Planning

Like all other aspects of your financial plan, the task of your planner will be to arrange the affairs of your estate in a manner consistent with your personal objectives. In establishing your objectives, there are really only two major considerations: (1) who should get what and how and when they should get it; and (2) how to avoid or minimize the taxing of your estate by the federal government, the state government, or both.

The best arrangement would be one in which all of your wishes could be achieved without Uncle Sam inheriting a penny. It is far more likely, however, that compromises will be required. Some of your wishes may have to be discarded unless you are willing to subject your estate to certain tax consequences, and some of your heirs may have to live with certain inheritance taxes in order for your wishes to be fulfilled.

The Disposition of Your Estate

Before you can dispose of your estate, you first must understand exactly what it is. Essentially, your estate consists of all tangible assets or property including your house, car, cash, jewelry, personal possessions, and so on, and all intangible assets or property such as life insurance, stocks, bonds, and so forth that you own at the time of your death. All of your property and assets will then pass to your heirs either through a process known as probate or through an operation of law.

Probate Estate

A probate estate is handled through the courts by the person or persons whom the deceased has directly or indirectly appointed to act as his or her personal representative. An example of a direct appointment is the naming of an executor in your will. An example of an indirect appointment is the designating of an estate administrator by the courts if no will exists.

There are several advantages and disadvantages to probate. On the negative side, until your estate has been settled in the courts no one may have access to any of the assets or property, except those assets that pass directly to the beneficiary through an operation of law, such as life insurance proceeds.

In addition to delays while the estate is being settled, there is also a cost factor to contend with. By the time court fees, attorneys' fees, executors' fees and sometimes accountants' fees have been paid, the gross value of the estate may have been reduced by an average of 4-to-8 percent. If the settling of the estate goes smoothly, then the time and cost factors may be minimal. However, if someone contests the will, or if other complications arise, the estate could be tied up for years; and the fees paid to the various parties could be staggering.

The third negative aspect of a probate estate is that probate files are open to the public. Consequently, anyone can ascertain the size and disposition of your estate.

However, probate does have its distinct advantages. First, assuming you leave behind a valid will you can appoint your own executor and distribute your assets exactly as you see fit (unless other laws such as those governing community property supersede your wishes).

Second, and most important of all, probate limits the amount of time during which someone can challenge the will and/or creditors can make claims on the proceeds of the estate. One thing your family doesn't need is a creditor popping up two or three years after your death demanding an unexpected and substantial payment.

Another advantage to probate is that the activities of your executor are supervised by the court. Obviously, this doesn't guarantee that your executor won't be able to pull the wool over the court's eyes and make off with a portion of your estate, but it certainly will make it very difficult for that individual to do anything illegal or offside.

Operation of Law

When there's a preexisting legal agreement, a number of assets and properties can pass directly to your heirs outside of the probate estate. For example, when a joint tenancy title exists prior to death, the assets or property of the deceased are automatically transferred to the survivor. If a husband and wife are joint tenants of a home or bank account, the surviving spouse will inherit automatically.

Another example of an operation of law is the proceeds of a life insurance policy. Provided a legal beneficiary has been designated, the life insurance proceeds pass to that beneficiary outside of the probate estate, which is why it is advisable to consider some form of life insurance. If your other assets are going to be tied up for a while until the estate is settled, the cash benefits from a life insurance policy may be the only capital your spouse and children will have to live on for many months.

Although passing property and assets to your heirs through an operation of law has its definite advantages, adequate forethought should be given before property titles are assigned or beneficiaries are appointed to avoid difficulty if your personal circumstances change over a period of time. Suppose when you were young and in love you automatically included you spouse in all of your financial affairs by opting for joint tenancy or co-ownership. Suddenly, after 15 years of marriage your spouse runs off with your best friend. Unless you can get all of these titles changed through another operation of law (e.g., a divorce agreement) your spouse would still be legally entitled to inherit all of these jointly held assets and properties in the event of your death. Or, if you name each child specifically as a co-beneficiary of your life insurance policy and forget to update your policy after the birth of your third child, only the first two children legally would be entitled to share the proceeds. Even if you thought you had all of the angles covered by wording the beneficiary clause to read "John, Mary, and all other children of this marriage," that phrase would still exclude any adopted children or any children from a former or future marriage. Worse still, if the spouse who ran off with your best friend was listed as the owner of the policy, you couldn't change the beneficiary designations if you wanted to.

This is not to say that you should keep every asset and every piece of property in your own name. It is merely to suggest that ample consideration should be given to possible future circumstances and consequences before selecting a specific title or form of ownership.

Estate and Inheritance Taxes

Whenever property or assets change hands the government expects its fair share—whether the taxpayers think it's fair or not. In the case of your estate, both the federal and the state government will be hoping to become one of your heirs. While the Federal government imposes taxes on the value of your estate, most state governments impose inheritance taxes on your heirs. Although it may be "more blessed to give than it is to receive," when it comes to estate planning, both giving and receiving are taxable by law. Since each state has its own inheritance tax laws, we highly recommend you consult with an estate expert to discuss the effects of state tax on your estate.

From the Federal government's perspective, your taxable estate is calculated as shown in Figure 13–1.

Figure 13–1
Your Taxable Estate

Your Gross Estate

Minus

a. Funeral/Burial Expenses
b. Administration Expenses
c. Marital Deduction
d. Charitable Deduction
e. Debts of Your Estate

Equals

Your Taxable Estate

1. **Your Gross Estate.** Your gross estate consists of all tangible and intangible assets and properties.

2. **Funeral/Burial Expenses.** There is no cap on the amount you can allocate or the funds your family can spend on your funeral and/or burial.

3. **Administration Expense.** This deduction includes all expenses pertaining to the settling of your estate, including fees paid to the probate court, lawyers, accountants, executors, trustees, and so forth.

4. **Marital Deduction.** In 1981, the federal tax code exempted all transfers of assets and/or properties from one spouse to another from both gift and estate taxes. Consequently, if your estate is passing in its entirety to your spouse, it would be completely deductible provided the following conditions are met:

   Your spouse must be entitled to all income from the assets or properties for life.

   Any income derived from your assets or properties must be paid to your spouse not less than once a year.

   No portion of any asset or property and no portion of any income from any asset or property can be granted to any other beneficiary during the lifetime of your spouse. In other words, you cannot give your stock portfolio to your spouse and then stipulate in your will that 50 percent of the proceeds from the portfolio are to be paid to your children. If you did, the portfolio would no longer be exempt under the marital deduction.

5. **Charitable Deduction.** There is no cap on the amount you can bequeath to charity through your estate.

6. **Debts of Your Estate.** Any amounts paid by your estate to various creditors will be deducted from your gross estate.

Avoiding or Minimizing Estate Shrinkage

As you can see, if your estate is passing in its entirety to your surviving spouse, estate taxes are not applicable. However, any properties or assets transferred to other beneficiaries such as your children at the time of your death or at the death of your surviving spouse will be taxed on any amounts in excess of $600,000.

Suppose, for example, your gross estate at the time of your death will be $850,000. In your will you have designated your spouse as your sole beneficiary, and he or she will be able to live entirely off the interest of the estate without having to tap into any of the principal (see Figure 13–2).

Since your entire estate is passing to your spouse, the total amount of $787,500 qualifies for the marital deduction. Therefore, no estate taxes would be incurred. Now, suppose your spouse has a will that designates the proceeds of his or her estate to pass to your children. Figure 13–3 illustrates the tax effect.

Although your spouse isn't going to touch any of the principal, by the time your children inherit the balance, your total estate will have been reduced by nearly 20 percent! The only way to avoid estate shrinkage is to plan the disposition of your assets in such a way as to avoid or minimize estate taxes and a second set of probate expenses. The most effective way to accomplish this end is through the use of trusts, lifetime gifts and/or estate equalization.

Figure 13–2
Your Estate After Expenses

Your Gross Estate		$850,000
Less:	Funeral/Burial Expenses	(10,000)
	Probate Costs (approx. 5%)	(42,500)
	Debts of Estate	(10,000)
Taxable Estate		$787,500

Figure 13–3
Spouse's Estate

Spouse's Gross Estate		$787,500
Less:	Funeral/Burial Expenses	(10,000)
	Probate Costs (approx. 5%)	(39,375)
	Debts of Estate	(1,000)
Taxable Estate		$737,125
Less:	Estate Tax Exemption	(600,000)
Total Taxable Estate		$137,125
Estate Tax (approx. 28%)		(38,395)
Total Value of Estate		$698,730

Trusts

For centuries people have used trusts as an effective means of holding, managing, and/or transferring various forms of property or assets. In order to establish a trust, the owner of the property or assets transfers the legal title to a designated trustee. The trustee is then obligated by law to manage the property for the benefit of the legally appointed beneficiary of the trust in strict accordance with the specific instructions outlined by the original owner.

Basically, all trusts belong to one or two categories: *inter-vivos* (living) trusts or *testamentary* trusts. The difference between the two is that the inter-vivos trust is valid during the lifetime of the individual who establishes the trust (the trustor), while the testamentary trust becomes valid at the time of the trustor's death.

Trusts offer a number of advantages, not the least of which is the ability to transfer all or any portion of your estate outside of probate. Since a trust passes assets to your beneficiaries through an operation of law, it is an effective way to prevent public disclosure of your estate. And, since a legally established trust allows assets to pass to your heirs outside of probate, your beneficiaries aren't going to have to wait several months or several years before they can use the proceeds of your estate.

Some trusts allow you to designate several generations of beneficiaries if you wish. For example, a *spousal remainder trust* entitles the surviving spouse to all of the income from your assets during his or her lifetime and then names the legal beneficiaries of that trust in the event of your spouse's death. By using this mechanism, your estate will still qualify for the marital deduction when it passes to your surviving spouse. In addition to giving you greater control over your estate beyond your lifetime, a trust of this kind also helps you to avoid the double-probate whammy. Using a trust rather than a will in the example given in Figure 13–3 could save your estate over $77,000 by eliminating all of the probate costs. Suppose you wanted to make sure all your hard-earned money went to your favorite charity rather than your worthless brother-in-law. You could establish a *charitable remainder trust* that would guarantee all the remaining assets of your estate would be transferred to the charity in the event of your spouse's death.

A trust can be an effective way of safeguarding your estate from mismanagement as well. For example, if your affairs are relatively complicated or require special expertise to manage them effectively, and your spouse is not up to the task, your estate could shrink dramatically with one or two wrong decisions. The person you appoint as the legal guardian of your minor children may not be a financial wizard either. By establishing a trust and appointing a trustee who is capable of managing your financial affairs profitably, both your surviving spouse and your minor children would be in far better financial condition.

When selecting the right form of trust for your estate-planning needs, be sure to weigh any possible tax benefits of an *irrevocable* (i.e., non-amendable) trust against the value of being able to maintain control of your assets during your lifetime through a *revocable* (amendable) trust. Personal and financial circumstances can undergo many changes in your lifetime, and you may wish to keep the trust as flexible as possible despite a potential loss in tax advantages.

Lifetime Gifts

One way of avoiding or minimizing estate taxes is to make lifetime gifts to your heirs. Currently, you can make an annual tax-free gift of up to $10,000 to anyone you wish. For example, if you have two children, both you and your spouse are eligible to make a $10,000 gift each year to each child. Consequently, you could make tax-free gifts of up to $40,000 a year to your two heirs.

Unfortunately, these gifts are not necessarily tax free forever. At the time of your death, these lifetime gifts are combined or unified with the portion of your taxable estate received by your heirs. For example, if you made lifetime gifts of $400,000 to one of your children and that same child also inherits $300,000 from your estate, in essence, this unified sum (less expenses and/or credits) would be used to determine the amount of taxes due to the federal government.

At face value, lifetime gifts don't appear to be much more than a means of delaying the inevitable. However, there are several definite tax advantages that make lifetime gifts very attractive. First, the taxable amount of the gift is based on the value of the gift at the time it was given. If you give someone stocks valued at $10,000, and the portfolio increases in value to $100,000 at the time of your death, the stocks are taxed at the value they possessed on the very day you gave them away—$10,000.

The second tax advantage to lifetime gifts is that in many cases any income or interest derived from such gifts will be taxed at a significantly lower rate. Since the donor (e.g., the parent) is generally in a much higher tax bracket than the donee (e.g., the child), these tax savings can be significant over the years. Lifetime gifts are most advantageous when they consist of various properties or assets that are likely to increase significantly in value over a period of time, such as stocks, bonds, real estate, and so forth.

Estate Equalization

The technique of estate equalization basically involves dividing up a large estate between two spouses in order to avoid or minimize taxes when the estate is transferred from the surviving spouse to the children.

Suppose your current net worth is approximately $800,000, and you are listed as the sole owner of all of your assets and properties. In the event of your death, your estate would pass directly to your spouse. Because of the marital deduction, there would be no tax consequences to this transfer. However, when your spouse dies and the entire estate is transferred to your child, approximately $200,000 of that estate will be subject to taxes.

The best way to avoid this situation is to divide up your estate more equally between yourself and your spouse during your lifetime. For example, if you listed your spouse as a joint owner, and listed your child as a beneficiary of the remainder of your estate, then at the time of your death, your spouse would inherit one-half of the estate ($400,000). Obviously, since the child's inheritance is below $600,000 no federal estate taxes would apply. Then, when your spouse passed on, the remainder of the estate ($400,000) would also pass tax-free to your child. Even if you are reluctant to transfer some percentage of your assets to your spouse during your lifetime, you can achieve the same results by using various living or testamentary trusts.[1]

[1]In 1987 the unified credit for estate and gift taxes is set at $192,800. Consequently, no estate or gift tax would be due unless the total gifts and transfers made during the husband's lifetime and at his death exceeded $600,000. With regard to his spouse, any money or property transferred by the husband to his wife, whether during his life or through his estate, is free from federal gift and estate tax provided:

1. the spouse is entitled to all income from the property for life.
2. the income from the property is paid at least once a year.
3. no one other than the spouse has the power to grant any portion of the property to any other person during the spouse's lifetime.

As you can see, there are a number of different estate-planning options that your planner may recommend in order to minimize the potential erosion of your estate through taxes or the various transfer costs associated with probate. Which of these alternatives you select will be entirely up to you. It is important, however, to do *something* about your estate plans—and to do it *now.*

Don't Underestimate the Value of Your Estate

When it comes to estate planning, the biggest mistake most people make is underestimating the value of their assets. Remember, when you sign your will, the bell doesn't automatically "toll for thee." There is an assumption of life expectancy that should also be factored into your estate plans. In fact, this is one of the rare times when inflation actually works in your favor. As an example, suppose you are 30 years old and Figure 13–4 is a list of your current assets:

Figure 13–4
Current Assets

Cash in Savings Account	$5,000
Automobile	10,000
Common Stocks	10,000
Personal IRA Account	8,000
Personal Residence	90,000
Vacation Property	25,000
Employee Pension Plan	5,000
Jewelry (gold watch/diamond ring)	6,000
Other Personal Property	10,000
Total Current Assets	$169,000

At the moment, there doesn't appear to be a great deal to divide among your heirs. And certainly no one is going to have to worry about paying estate taxes—or so it would seem. However, according to the mortality tables, you can probably anticipate another 40 years of life. Imagine what the value of your estate would be if you continued to add to your assets while inflation continued to increase their value year after year. Imagine the value of your real estate in 40 years. Imagine what can happen to the prices of gold and diamonds. Your long-term growth stocks may seem inconsequential at the moment, but what might they be worth in another decade or two? In 40 years your estate could well be worth over a million dollars!

When planning your estate, there must be a careful blending of current and future expectations. Your plans must reflect your current personal wishes, and they must reflect also the future value of your assets. Most important of all, whenever your personal or financial circumstances change, your estate plans must be flexible enough to keep pace with the unexpected. As we mentioned earlier, it might be better to keep your options open in the short term at the possible expense of future estate taxes than to write your final wishes in concrete. Don't try to resolve the matter of your estate once and for all. Your estate should be arranged so that, with periodic revisions, you can take care of your family in the event of your premature death as well as be sufficiently flexible to take care of your family should you live a long and prosperous life.

THE SENSE

Providing your family and loved ones with financial security is certainly important, but it is equally important to provide for their emotional support as well.

No amount of money or property can compensate a child for the loss of a beloved parent or a spouse for the loss of a lifetime lover, friend, and companion. No amount of estate planning can compensate for this emotional blow either. What you can do, however, is to minimize the circumstances your family will have to contend with in the event of your death by making a number of important decisions during your lifetime.

1. **Who Will Look After Your Children?** If you and your spouse were both involved in a fatal accident, who would look after your minor children? Remember, unless you legally appoint someone as their guardian, the court will make this decision for you.
2. **Who Will Look After Your Affairs?** When selecting an executor for your estate, the tendency is to choose your spouse, a relative, or a close friend of the family. Unfortunately, this is not always the best choice to make. In the first place, anyone who is this close to you during your lifetime is going to be experiencing a great deal of emotional turmoil at the time of your death. The fact is, he or she simply may not be able to cope with the burden of settling your affairs for many, many months.

   Moreover, the executor of your estate has a number of highly complicated legal and tax matters to contend with, including filing various tax returns and tax forms, determining the value of your estate, settling debts with your creditors, and so forth. All of these affairs require someone with a clear head and a degree of financial expertise. For this reason, you might consider the advisability of naming your attorney, your bank, or your accountant as the executor or coexecutor of your estate.
3. **Last Wishes.** One of the things that can give your loved ones a great deal of comfort is the knowledge that they are following your last wishes to the letter. As difficult as it is to do, be sure your family and friends have a clear sense of how you would like your burial or funeral to be conducted. The

more specific you are, the easier it will be for them to make the necessary arrangements. Do you want a notice to appear in the local newspaper? Do you want friends to make donations rather than send flowers? Do you want a headstone or a simple plaque? These are just a few of the dozens and dozens of details that should be addressed clearly.

4. **Access to Important Documents.** Ask yourself this question: If you were to die today, would your spouse or heirs know exactly where to find your will? Your insurance policies? Your stock portfolio? Your bank accounts? Trying to piece together all of this information during your lifetime is enough of a nightmare—as you will soon discover when your planner asks you to assemble this information. It is an unimaginable horror when someone has died unexpectedly.

   Take the time right now to draw up a simple list of all your assets and properties as well as the location of all important documents. Then, as your financial circumstances change throughout the years, update the list as required. You have no idea what a blessing this simple document will be to your family.

5. **Emotional Support.** Be sure to discuss with your family the various people they should turn to in the event of your death in addition to relatives and friends. A family lawyer, for instance, can provide immeasurable comfort to a grieving spouse. Just knowing that someone is there who will handle the burden of settling the estate can make a world of difference. Is there someone in particular they should call upon to make the funeral arrangements? Is there a person they should contact to handle all of the tax matters? Who should they turn to for financial advice? Moral support? Spiritual comfort?

In order to plan your estate effectively, you may have to give a great deal of thought to matters that many of us would prefer to avoid. For this reason, it may be helpful to remember that estate planning ultimately centers around the issue of life, not death, since your estate plans will guarantee a certain measure of financial support and emotional comfort to your family for the rest of their lives.

Exercise 13–1
Working with Your Planner—Summary Checklist

Before

( ) Prepare a complete list of all your current assets, properties, and holdings, as well as the location of all valuable documents.

( ) Give consideration to all of the financial and emotional objectives you would like to achieve.

( ) Assemble all pertinent estate-planning documents, including your will or any trusts you have already established.

( ) If you are planning to name a particular family member or friend as your executor, or as the legal guardian of your children, or as a trustee or co-trustee for your estate, be sure to discuss this issue with that individual and obtain his or her consent.

During

( ) Do not make any irrevocable commitments in haste. It might be more advisable to sacrifice certain tax benefits in order to maintain control over your assets.

( ) It may be wise to discuss the planner's recommendations with an estate attorney or other specialists in this field.

(continued)

Exercise 13–1 continued

( ) If the planner has consulted with an estate specialist in the development of your plan, examine the credentials and the reputation of the specialist closely before you follow his or her advice.

( ) Be aware of the costs involved with any course of action you are considering. For example, trusts have specific start-up costs and annual maintenance fees that should be weighed against possible probate costs. Also, depending on the complexity of the trust you select, there may be substantial accounting fees involved as well.

( ) Be sure your estate plans reflect not only the current value but also the future value of your assets and properties.

( ) Do not take chances with your estate. Select an executor and/or a trustee who is knowledgeable and trustworthy.

After

( ) Your estate plans should be reviewed on a regular basis (at least every three to five years).

( ) Update your estate plans immediately whenever there is a change in your financial or personal affairs.

( ) If you acquire additional properties, be certain that the manner in which you designate ownership is consistent with your estate plans.

14
Implementing Your Decision

Several thousand years ago there lived among the Greeks two great orators named Cicero and Demosthenes. History has it that when Cicero spoke the crowds would applaud loudly saying, "What a great speech Cicero has given." The record also shows that when Demosthenes addressed an audience the gathering would cheer wildly saying, "Let us march!"

Hopefully, when you reach the end of this book you will not simply lay it to one side saying, "My, what an informative book that was." Instead, we hope the information you found in these pages will cause you to take some immediate and affirmative action.

Unfortunately, simply being well informed about the financial-planning process is not going to fix the future. In fact, sometimes being well informed about a particular subject can lead to disastrous consequences. Like an anesthetic, information may tend to mask painful circumstances temporarily rather than prompting you to get to the root of the problem once and for all.

Suppose, for example, your best friend has just had a serious heart attack. Since you are approximately the same age as your friend, you become deeply concerned about your own physical condition. As a result, you begin to attack your fears by sitting down with a best-selling book on jogging. The danger is that by the time you have finished the book and become an armchair expert on the topic of physical fitness, you are so enthralled with your newfound knowledge that you never quite get around to actually jogging. Oh, you might go so far as to buy a new pair of running shoes and perhaps even a stop watch to monitor your pulse rate; but somehow, now that you *know* the solution, you fail to take the necessary steps to actually *do* something practical about it. In the final analysis, if the money and time you have invested in this book are to have any value at all, you must take immediate action.

STEP ONE: YOUR DECISION

The first thing you must do is to decide, once and for all, whether personal financial planning is for you. In Chapter 1 you were asked to complete a questionnaire and to use the scoring key to identify the extent to which personal financial planning might be of benefit to you and your family. This questionnaire, combined with all of the exercises you were asked to complete and information you were given in subsequent chapters, should be sufficient to give you a clear sense of where you stand financially.

Actually, this should be a very simple decision. There are no gray areas in financial planning. Either you are in excellent financial shape or you aren't. If you have a good handle on your financial affairs and are tracking nicely along a well defined financial course, quite frankly, personal financial planning would be a waste of your time and your money. (If you are already in excellent health, why go to another doctor for a second opinion?)

However, if you do not feel completely confident about your current or future financial well-being, then you must take corrective steps immediately by taking advantage of the financial planning process.

Suggestion: In the spaces that follow, write the decision you have made regarding your need for financial planning as well as the reasons you have made this particular decision. Transferring your mental thoughts to writing will help to clarify and firmly establish your decision.

Decision: ____

Reason(s): ____

____

____

____

____

STEP TWO: SELECTING YOUR PLANNER

In Chapter 2 we discussed all of the key factors to consider in the selection of a competent financial planner. The one thing we didn't tell you, however, was where to find one!

Whether you opt for a commission planner, a fee planner or a fee plus commission planner, there are several organizations that can assist you in your search including:

International Association of Financial Planners
2 Concourse Parkway, Suite 800
Atlanta, GA 30328
(800) 241-2148

Institute of Certified Financial Planners
3443 South Galena, Suite 190
Denver, CO 80231-5093
(303) 751-7600

You might also wish to contact the Board of Certified Public Accountants in your state or a local chapter of the American Bar Association. (If you have trouble locating a local chapter, contact the national headquarters of the American Bar Association in Chicago, Illinois at (312) 988-5158.) Inquiries may also be directed to the Securities Exchange Commission in New York if you wish to ascertain that your financial planner is a registered stockbroker or to the Chartered Life Underwriters Association if you need a planner with expertise in the insurance field. Your local banker, your family lawyer, or accountant can also be of assistance in making recommendations. Remember, the quality of the planner you select will ultimately determine the quality of the plan you receive. Don't settle on the first name you receive or the first person you interview.

Suggestion: One of the best ways to overcome procrastination is to establish a specific plan with a specific deadline. In the spaces that follow, write your deadline date for selecting your personal financial planner. Then list the names and telephone numbers of the organizations or individuals you intend to contact immediately to begin the search.

Deadline Date: ______________________________

Contact: ______________________ Phone: __________

Contact: ______________________ Phone: __________

Contact: ______________________ Phone: __________

Contact: ______________________ Phone __________

Contact: ______________________ Phone: __________

STEP THREE: DEVELOPMENT OF YOUR PLAN

Once you have selected your planner, follow the recommendations and guidelines we have outlined in Chapter 3 regarding the financial-planning process. Be sure to monitor carefully the steps your planner is taking and provide as much information and assistance as you can. The more specific you are about your financial affairs and your personal goals, the better equipped the planner will be to get the job done to your complete satisfaction.

Suggestion: If you have not already done so, be sure to complete all of the exercises in this book. Completing these exercises will help you develop a clearer sense of your current financial situation as well as your long-term objectives.

STEP FOUR: IMPLEMENTING YOUR PLAN

Once you are thoroughly satisfied with the direction and the recommendations of your plan, be certain you follow through and actually implement those recommendations. Once again, don't get lulled into a false sense of security simply because your financial well-being looks assured on paper. Until you actually purchase the insurance, invest in the stocks, deposit the funds into an IRA, set up the trust for your heirs, and so forth, you aren't any better off financially than you were before your plan was developed!

Suggestion: Establish a deadline date for implementing each recommendation your planner makes. Ask your planner to assist you in making sure that each recommendation is implemented in a thorough and timely manner.

STEP FIVE: REGULAR REVIEW

Always remember that your financial plan must be kept current. Rather than waiting for a specific event to occur that suggests the need to review your plan—such as a raise in pay or a dramatic dip in the stock market—why not also establish some regular "check-up" dates as soon as your plan has been completed? You should have your plan reviewed at least once a year. However, it might be a good idea to plan a review every six months for the first two years to make certain that the course your planner has charted for you is really taking you in the right direction.

If you have ever watched a navigator on a ship or an airplane, you will notice that they keep checking and rechecking their course several times an hour, the reason being that the sooner they detect an error and correct it, the easier it is to get back on track. Left unchecked, a ship or a plane that is veering a few degrees off course throughout the entire journey will end up hundreds of miles away from its targeted destination. The same is also true of financial planning. If you identify the need for a slight course correction fairly early in the game, then the error can usually be fixed in a matter of weeks or months. However, if you fail to notice that a particular stock is not performing as well as it should be or that the inflation rate has risen slightly higher than anticipated, and if that problem goes uncorrected for several years, you could find yourself thousands of dollars away from *your* targeted destination.

Suggestion: Ask the planner to list specific six-month review dates in the implementation section of the plan. Then ask the planner to send you reminder notices well in advance of the dates to assure that you don't overlook these important sessions.

Finally, if you have decided to make personal financial planning a part of your life and if you have followed through on each of the critical steps outlined in this book, then may we suggest one final step? Do what Cicero and Demosthenes probably did after each of their great speeches—congratulate yourself for a job well done!

Index